MY WAY, THE TRUTHFUL WAY

TANYA TURTON

Copyright © 2022 Tanya Turton

Copyright remains the property of the author and apart from any fair dealing for the purposes of private study, research, criticism or review, as permitted under the Copyright Act, no part may be reproduced by any process without written permission. All inquiries should be made to the author.

Typeset & Cover by Chain of Hearts Creative

National Library of Australia - ISBN-978-0-6452064-4-9

THIS INTERPRETATION OF LIFE AS IT IS SEEN BY ME.

{Tanya; the author and receiver of these channellings}

I am willing, am I not to express this version of me for all to see?

Yes, it appears to be true, but I ask this of myself. Was this version that I have been offering outwardly, really me.

For you see and those of you that know me or think to know of me as this one that they are to see or recognise me as their version of myself to see. Let it be offered here that in spirits words offered; are we ever *'the real version'* to be sharing or speaking.

Let me explain; for it has been made clear to me in all that I have received in many conversations, writings, channellings, and meditation sessions that I now can look back upon or reflect into that I now know that just maybe I have not been true to ME.

This I hear the many of you asking, why? How did this become apparent to you?

I felt it. I respond in this version of myself that I interact into and out of with today that now I know that of what it was that I offered to not only myself but you as well I was not being true or real to me.

This has been an arduous task shall I call it of that, to have started when I became an envisionment of this self to see, yes it was a desire of mine to call unto myself to embed into my very being of spirited essence that I was to be allowing of myself to exist as.

This continuation into not only this life as human form now but the many, many that have existed before me as Tanya perse` in this life to interact into. For I have become many contributions I will call of them as this to be a student of the universe, the philosophy of life to exist into in this realm and the many that exist outside of this existence that I am here and now. You are the chooser of all this that one is to see, and we have offered this to many in recorded literature, ancient texts, spoken verbal offerings and writings to be spoken of in this way. So, it is a truthful knowing that the many of you are to exist into here and now in a truth that you are not receiving of words or knowledge with which you do not really resonate. Is it?

We introduce ourselves as the beings of Love & Light in which it is that this human responds to or interacts into when conversations or moments of trust and gracious receiving's are felt.

Be allowing of us to embark upon this journey of discovering you with you and the all that you shall always be known to us as. In here we wish to offer this reasoning that is to flow up and out of you in this human casement to be called as uniquely your own to be this establishment that you have drawn up or requested shall we say to be felt as needed by you to be this one as YOU. You have required and deeply desired this version of you to be this envisionment of self to be, for it has been a yearning or asking out of much love to be felt by you to feel this interpretation rise.

> *Note: It is you that we ask to stop of what it is that you are doing (reading) get up and go and take a look at this physical being of expression to be that you are; if you can or feel inclined to do so.*

What is it that you saw, what are the first words that you responded with in regard to this vision of self to see? What did the mirror reflect back to you? but more importantly what did this human version of yourself, the old seer of you offer you to see, hear or know?

Can you feel the judgement from within this being that you are to respond to self in this old way, we need to correct here, just maybe you love of all that you see and are never to judge or place criticism upon thee? Then if this is you, we can feel of this to celebrate you from within this being that you are to interpret yourself as, this is great!

But if on the other hand it was not the image or words that you were hoping to see or utter than we suggest to you to continue into these pages with us to feel as a willingness from within to hear of all that we in you have to relay.

Content spoken about in this book
{Chapter 8} may cause a heightened response
within self, sadness and an upset to those
that are sensitive to this matter in regard to
self harm, suicidal thoughts and tendencies
and the deciding that loved ones choose
to end their life upon this earthly plane.

Please read only if felt guided towards.

^ We honour this channel in her receiving
of this offering as hard to receive, it is
written with a knowing of another to have
been to offer all this to explain. It is to
throw light on the passing of a human
by self to explain. Self-harm to end of
one's life is spoken of in an honest and
open way in this passage to be received.

CHAPTER 1

THE LOVED VERSION OF YOU

In this we wish to share; it is you that is always the version of a loving being to recognise you as.

You are this grand version of love that we speak to, to become a willing voice from out of you to hear yourself speak of and as. Let it be spoken of here that we are to be the interjectors {if to call us to be that} we are upon your connection to this that you really are, this voice of wisdom that you link into, this being of love and light that you suddenly discover or intuitively become asking of to see, and we offer you will.

In a response to be felt as if to flow out of you to ask this of self to know.

Am I really this way to see myself as? Love & Light.

Why would one not see oneself in this way, we ask?

Let it be offered here in a plain & straightforward way as to be interpreted by you to hear; this that you speak of as you, has lived into many conversations, versions, and interpretations of this self to be, has she/ he not? It is in their deliberate being of human physicality that you have enabled not only yourself but the many of others that are viable to you to think of as important judgers of you to be that you have become a response to. Let down your guard here in this position of which it is that you are to feel as though it is of us to judge you in this place as to not really know you . We do!! For we are every version and aspect of you to see and interact into and out of. This is hard to determine or receive yes, we know, but in all that is and is not physical to see of as determined yet to have been or is, it is in this etherical existence that all is to become, so in a deeper level to undermine you it feels, honestly spoken we are you and are to know of you intimately well, that we suggest,

We are you.

It is in this determining that ones such as you are to be placing self into a space of self-recognition to become a clearer more evolved being of love and light that you desire to be. It is in this eternal being of love that you are that you are willing to venture further out onto the branch to call it of this to suggest how far one will go to learn, live into, become, and try out shall we say to be a bolder grander version of this soul lighted spirit that you are in truth to be.

So let us offer here, YES! you are a human form no doubt about that for this is all that you see and feel, is it not?

You are the eliminators of the internalness, the gods voice, the intrinsic self to have been established and enabled by this soul gifted you to have been to become, and it is in the denying of this self to be really honest in a true and thoughtful way as to of really what it is that you are or exist as, it is then in the rediscovering of the all that you are in us as you to be that you will find a harder processing or thought concept to interact or accept as yours to learn again or to even want to know or recognise into again.

Let us accompany you here along this pathway of enlightenment {it is this word that many of you as humans choose this journey to be named} for yes you are all striving from a deeper response within to feel this journey or life as an achievement to become known to us again.

Appear as not to be shocked by the words that we offer, for if it is your first time to come into contact with words or thoughts such as these it will be we offer a hard placement of self to sit into. For to hear of self as not really this that you are in physical is challenging, is it not? Appearing in a way as if to almost disqualify the human that you be. Know this is not our intent to distract you or drag you off your pathway of enlightenment that you may be currently on, but we will say it is here that you are hoping of self to find, is it not?

To be asking of this one in human to find love, feel love or recognise love in self again, is this not of why it is that you reached for this book to maybe just maybe find suggestions into how to find love for self again.

Let us be honest in this that we always speak of as truth to be, we are this establishment that is to rival you, {the human you} to feel as a response that is to rage from deeply within you to think of self as another way!

What we hear you express;

I think, I am going mad.

<u>NO! you are not,</u> let us speak to the you that is the seer, the searcher from within, the voice that enables you to feel this real love as yours. It is your soul-based identity that is you that we wish to speak to, for she is recognising of all in this that we be, for she is of this that we all are complete.

You are to be willing we ask to sit in a place of receivership to learn, to master, to forgive, to acknowledge of all in this that we are to speak.

We know of you all so well. It is in this forming of self that you decided to become just this time around for it is to be spoken of the many contributions that you have existed into to gain, learn, experience, and master this soulful decision to be that you are.

In human physicality there is immense pressure placed upon oneself as if to strain or drain the entire existence out of you that you really are. Humans as interactive beings on a physical denser level are so devoted it appears to misinterpretations of this self to be and are willing in many if not most opportunities to interact with others that appear to know you better than you. Is this not correct to ask?

You in this self has and it has been a requirement by you not on a soul level but this earthly being level that you requested of it as so.

Let us describe; To be non-coherent to spirit or exist in a sleepened state as another version of self to think into than this one was to become the ruler of thee. This heavy dense form of life as you know it to be your human structure to see.

So, it is here that we offer that the loved version of you is the bold glowing light, the daring show pony, the envisioners of only love to be that we see as you.

It is not the human dread or anxious nervousness, the despair, or the hated version that you see, the one that you do not allow self to connect into for fear of what it is that you will see, and discover to reveal as real you, this is not where we lay.

It is in the bold extravagant version of you to respond into this life with such oomph and contagious glee to explode and feel accepting of all that you see to be ME(you).

Here is where you will find us.

You are this ME that we see, she is an exquisite being of love and light shielded and hidden out of view by the human contraption that is you. Let us offer very well intended we say to experience into this life as you to be though. For she/ he knew of all that he has come here decided to be, yes it may not feel like that in a human thought to process, but the interjection of spirit that you are, the willing passenger that we be in you, knows of your obvious weaknesses, failures or strengths and contributions to be offered here in this form of life to exist into, but it is in all this that you display to accept or place before you that you are to be to become this learned version of you. Many lessons lay apparent and extravagant in equal accepting of good and bad as you see of them to be expressed by you to see, let it be spoken of here in this your now that they all shall be yours to own up to or answer to and review upon your return back to thee {Home}.

So let it be offered here that this loved being that you strive into or are searching of to be, you are even more in grander way than you could ever imagine in a human thought to allow of self to see, to feel, to know.

Are you suggesting that I AM not ME?

In a way to suggest YES, for many of you have lived since birth a challenged space of recognition to become, all totally designed by you to feel this expression of self as to be in a contrast or not of what it is that you really are or like to be. So yes, very warranted we offer.

Let this not confuse you, for oh` you of human identity will have taken this earthly life force to the extreme in a relationship to call of it as your own, one that you have endeavoured to express to this self and many that you interact with as hell upon this earth, have you not?

So many of you have been eager to be, and you did exactly that, you became this unseeing version of the real you to see. Let down your eagerness to strive into a version of you that you are not and allow for this self to become the keen understander of and in all this that you are to know yourself to be. If not in this state of which it appears to comprehend from a human state of recognition but in one that will empower you to thrust yourself into this divine being of love that you are to recognise of self once more.

This love that you speak of sounds foreign to me. Why?

It is only out of the unlovable you that you have allowed of self to become or transition into that you will feel of this statement to come forth.

You are willing are you not, we ask?

Willing of what ??? I ask.

To be this abandonment of this hardened self in physical form; to suggest to self to be in a willingness to love in all that you be once more, to recognise this self as the holder only of the magnificent truth that you be defined in purpose as `GRAND LOVE` to be.

I LOVE ME. Do I not?

In this your realisation to speak of as an image or viewing of this self to be you will feel this to respond to as a NO! (in most we receive this honest reply)

In all reality you as in most pretend to love this self, talking oneself into this relationship and pretending to care and offering outwardly empty robotically repeated dullened words that hold no anticipation or devoted feelings of LOVE. It is only because the literature and learnings of your current NOW has guided you there.... But we ask this of you; Do you really genuinely LOVE YOU?

We watch in LOVING presence` YOU this being of strict human trying to LOVE this version of you and in this we offer to speak a dedication in many at their persistence that they partake into.

But let us offer here to say that in one's version that you are to be partaking into now you are just this perception of self to be. You have been living a lie it appears to be told by yourself here to speak that you have existed in many forms as such in comparison or relation to those that you know of as yours to interact with.

Let all asking this question, be able and willing in a generous suggestion to speak or hear this answer as a truth that is to be no longer denied within you as to the real you to answer this question of self to ask.

You are this love, let it be the interpreter into and of all that one is to see. Let it be your voice of recognition that you are to hear and feel, as this love that you are is to invade all if not every-thing that is this that you be and not.

CHAPTER 2

WE ARE, AS YOU ARE.

**Being found in this recognition
is a love of you to see.
You are the description of self to suggest to be.
Let this grand version, be yours to speak.
You know of this love as complete.
Be felt as to respond to only
a love so grand to see.**

Imagine this version of you

in all that you can.

You speak so willingly in this that I be you, why?

This we offer; you are.

There is to be no other comprehension, comparison, or suggestion to be felt by you as an offering so grand to call of self as this in us to be. The ever-diligent viewers of this that you be to always be felt as this instigation from within to call forth out of you a recogniser in this self to be you in this that we be.

We ask the many that are to connect into this way as to be calling forth out of you a wisdom so wise to speak that you cannot feel of it to be deceit or untruth, can you?

Let go of all hesitations upon the entering of this realm of thought to progress further into to ask of this self to see. You must be willing to sit into another frame of mind shall we say to comprehend this position within you to be speaking out of. You are this love that is you to be and in this way that we speak to offer it is never of another that we seek to find you in.

Let yourself speak in only love to be prevailed to all that you can for they are to hear of this advertisement that you are to extrude love into all that one is to be. You are this loving version of us in this extremity of self to see, you must in this instance know of this self to be a worthy opponent to live into as human recognition to see, to become this grand adventurer of the all that one was and is in hope to see.

I am unable to feel this comparison of you as 'I,' why?

It is simply in ones denying from within and the thinkers mind to project outwardly this imagery that one cannot possibly be this splendid.

In human form the many that we observe are to be disrespecting as in unknowing of the soul, the light, the vision that you are and if to put it straight, you are ignorant to this for a reason to become known by thee.

You are all hidden aspects of this that we are and in a realisation that is to escape from within to ask this question in or of a deeper level to answer, then and only then will one feel this as a responsible response to speak.

You are a beloved being of love and light and are caught often in this contraption of human form to sink into, feeling strangled and smothered as to the allowing of the real emergence of YOU.

I feel to ask more on this subject LOVE.

Yes, we honour this within thee to be responding to this question as it is to arise, for you see not all of you are to become apparent of this state of you that lives and dwells within as to be another to see, hear or be.

Let us guide you; hear to offer that it appears to many that this dwelling from within is to take on another form or personality to be, is this correct to ask of you to require an answer to?

Yes, it is often spoken of the many such as you that feel as to be different or assuming of self to be inhabited by another form or a different matter or energy. Let us offer to correct you of this; it is this matter that you speak of to be that you are, and it is the human configuration that you are to place first as a suggestion to be that you are not.

In this one to speak you are the version of this self to have become an establishment or a conditioning to be felt as you in human form but the many of you that interact here now in this that we be are to be becoming of a new truth to accept as themselves to be far greater and more advanced into an understanding of this that you are more.

Let us speak on this matter a little more. You are willing to interpret yourselves as more, are you not? Then let it be spoken of as this; you are the conducive version of this one to be an inhabitant upon this planet to experience life as an interaction with many, to be forgotten of the life, love or light that lives intently within having been placed there in your absoluteness of this self to be expressed as a star version or being of this self to be. You are knowing of this grandness upon your opening from within that speaks to you, in a voice and of this we have spoken before, a voice that you do not recognise or are startled at as time goes by.

Yes, I have heard this voice on several occasions spoken of by others. Will I hear this voice as my own?

In this entirety that you are to be, you will.

Yes, it is in this form that you are or have chosen of self to be that you are the certainty to become this that you sensed into self to respond to. So, let your voice be one of wonderment that is to catch you by surprise if to be spoken in and of love and to be never ruled or governed by this of another other than you. For it is this voice that is enticed purely by love when offered the platform to speak of all that you must stand upon to hear your voice once more as yours. You are willing we ask you of this ?

I hesitate to say Yes, for I am not sure I have the strength, belief, dedication or even the inclination to hear.

> Then let us offer that in this way present to speak, you will not.

It is a governing rule by the universal laws and the all that be the entirety of self in real version of self to speak as this soul offering that is you. It is a voice that is required by you to honour and accept to trust once more as the real speaker that defines you.

> We suggest a belief in you is required^

I feel this validation from within that you speak in truth to me.

It is to be always an acceptance by you in you that you are to carry yourself to be a willingness to hear it as your truth or not. This revealing in all aspects of this self to be.

Do you need to question
another to hear your own truth?
Are you willing to sit into this
receptive version of you to
feel your way as your own?
Can you hear this strength behind or
in this voice to call of it as your own?
Are you willing to interpret all that speak as
needed by you or not?
Does your current voice ring true to you?

Let yourself seek not of another to find this
voice of truth but to only pause to offer
your voice as a loudness in certainty to be.

My voice is as yours, are you offering this to me?

In a certain understanding of this to be
yes, we suggest this to be correct.

When one in human form can acknowledge a power of belief into this that they be to never need to question this self again. To be felt as this strong contender into a love felt heart speak to speak, then and only then will you feel this in us that you are to be. We are the recognisers of all as correct and right, and to be never to judge of another as them self to speak to feel not a need to argue or attain a vision of self to be seen as different or not the same. You are this envisionment of us in this that one is to be, so close of your eyes dear one and speak of this heart that is to express in only love so deep to be felt and you will hear this voice as yours in ours to be.

We recognise this light in you.

This is often heard as to suggest that I am a lighted being, why?

Is it not of this that you know?

Why in any other reason than to suggest as this that you are not knowing yet of your power that you possess.... would you not be willing to see this self so bright as to stand into a light that guides you, that becomes you, that enters you as this divinity of knowing from within all that becomes to be that IS.

We love of you dear ones in this present place of which it is that we appear to interact. So let of self be this divine intervention that has thus far captured your human spirit to respond to this question to rise and ask....

WHO & WHAT AM I?

This question is a commonly asked query as to the life that I live into and of what it is that I am here to achieve?

Know this dear one it is and in this to respond to you, we offer,

YOU ARE.....

`A spirited version of you, the soul existence that you be so divinely intertwined into and has great intend for you to become another version and another version of this self to see, to become this radiating version of love encumbered to be always in remembrance of this that we be. So, know of us to speak this way as to startle the many of you at times, which are to feel as though change is apparent or disbelief is to cloud your view, but you are a truth seeker, a finder of heart intended, and a voice that loves you to speak, and in this you will.`

Am 'i' entering into another version or dimension of myself, is this correct to ask?

Dear one you have and always will be this you.

But to question this self like this; than we shall respond that you are this version of you yes, but with a deep desire attached to find the real you. Many if not most are to bring with them a life intended lesson or yearning of self to grow more into, hence this explains the unsatiable thirst to be better, more generous, loved more, to feel sadder, more unloved, more/ or less greedy, less or/ more extravagant, alone, richer, poorer or dis at ease with this human form, it is in many requirements that you have landed here with. To call of these as a lesson for one's soul it shall remain to be spoken of as this to be. You are the human tester to become to feel, be willed into or out of and to exhibit this extreme learning pattern to become.

> *{It is to offer that all lessons received in earthly human experience are to contribute to the greater consciousness to become a furthering for the total being of love that exists as us in you}.*

Many speak of this earthly life as challenging. WHY?

This life dear one is a consideration to be called your own and if to be unloved or loveable by self than it shall. All being desired by you as you to become more.

As if in a comparison to the existence that is truly YOU in every aspect of this that you be, it is to offer there is no comparison or description that can or could equate to the trueness that lays eternally blessed within the all that source IS.

You speak of love as all that one needs, why are we to search of it?

Shouldn't it just be?

You are love this you are to know, but you as in many have come here with confusion and forgetfulness attached, to be constantly driven in this quest to serve others and to be a willed contender of not this love to be. You are all the powerful essence enriched of love and this was always a certainty to be, not the crowd driven way in which it is that you live upon this planet as to not be willing to see your own truth or to be felt misguided by this knowing self and to allow for all interferences be felt as required, than we say you shall not feel this love until you do decide to step out from behind the crowd, these ones that rule you as they think you should do and when this you do. You will hear a voice so divinely placed into you and then and only then will you speak this love for you in all that you be, say and do.

I feel to request this voice of mine to step forth.

Then of this it shall.

CHAPTER 3

FINDING MY WAY

To follow of another is to never serve you this we say, yes in one's ability to learn of this that they be they {as in you} will certainly try. It is to feel as not yet to trust into this that you be, does it not?

How many of you have requested another to offer, or to provide this love or a certainty to thee?

It is a given or an intended belief upon this planet that the many of you are to do, to fall heavily for another or become dependent upon another to live for. TO be the hearers of your governors or rulers, leaders, and lovers to express that one must do as I do and to not suggest another way to live.

You are all willing passengers here to be expressed to feel this dormant self that has become enslaved or captured by others as to be not yours to hear, let alone even recognised any more. Let oneself feel this to settle to know this that you be the leader within that speaks of only this love that you are to be. Let down your hesitation to turn things upon its tail or to take another view or response into of how it is that you are to think or be. It is often a contention from within that one will disappoint or not feel a strength to be willing to suggest that you would rather travel alone or upon another route or consider another option, than follow or conform. Is it not?

> You are many in this conformity it is that we are to see. WHY we ask?

Can one not think for themselves? Have you become so lost that a herding is needed to be?

You are the truth finders amongst yourselves to see, to be the eliminators of unjust and resist to the many that try and lead you or mould to conform you. It is in this becoming of which it is that you did that you would become a follower until this voice of love appeared to speak to you as so.

To find your own way.

I ask this of you spirit, am I not finding my own path then if I am to be questioning this to be you?

By this are you to mean us in spirit? YES.

We will offer you this; Let it be spoken as not all that feel to be lost are, and in this asking to become it is with a certainty that you know that you will.

So, you see, it is not of ours to concern we with, for all that ask to find their own way will. It is to be a path or journey that many will travel in a human way as to explain as to be searching for more of them to see. You are all looking for love, are you not? in no uncertain way whether it be a loved one to hold, a remembering of one loved to have passed, a love of self or even such a great distaste or dissatisfaction of love that this too becomes an asking of unloved to be the experience.

We would offer that the greatest journey that will unfold is of how and why it is that love is to be found and known by you?

Why are you to offer love as the ultimate lesson?

Love is a becoming dear one that you became of. It was to have birthed you into this recognition that you see existing here to see.

Was it not out of this grand love for self to envision that you became? maybe not always in a human response to love as it to be felt but in your truthful desire as your soul to express love in you, this you did.

It is to be a consideration here
in this your NOW, what is your
expectation of LOVE to be spoken of
by you as to see, feel or know?

Answer with truth intact and be willing to open ones heart in an honest, raw, deliberate and truthful way to respond to this question we ask.

Are you willing to dive deeper with us, we ask?

One is to be always this envisionment of love to be or not, are they not?

It is to dive deeper than one has ever imagined to feel as to enter into this regimented façade that you hold self into. Let go of these hardened visions of self to be perceived as not. Let all be a deciding from within to be calling forth this wisdom out of you to feel this love that is yours as a certainty to become. You are knowing of us here in this space to be calling out a deliberate essence of this self to become, for it is of you that we are to see. In an allowance of one to speak to the heart, this heart space that is to be thought of as to hold your love for self into in this entirety to be, be willing to release the demons of the human self to feel, to see, to witness, to forgive and to reject in and of the all that does not serve you to day. You are the visionary that volunteered to become this element of self to see, so it was of you to know of the exact time as such to call it of that to be that you will release all that you are not and allow in all that you are.

I AM WILLING, THIS I KNOW

In this we know.

It is to speak of it in this way that all that are to become this knowing to hear ones voice speak in a sense of a religious aspect to be heard, to remember the calling to self that one has made to be the ever diligent being of light and love from within to be always a remembering of this that you are to carry so that you may feel as this space of awareness opens into an entirety of this self to believe into as this in us that you be.

We offer you here this to receive that you are this loving energy that has always known of self to be this spark, this essence of god himself, this generated being of love to feel as to be an entirety from within to need no explanation of this love to be titled or described of it to be, for it is a wordless love that can and will be an expression of you in this extravagant being of the all that is. It is a response within you that has been called to surface to make a noticeable appearance so that you can see and witness of it once more, so that you will be the true receiver of all that is and will be.

You speak encouraging of this love as mine to be, why?

It is dear one.

If one is to not dive into self to look than it is of nothing to reveal.

It will be left to feel dormant in a sensing of this self to discover all that you asked of this self to be. To be ignorant to the love boldly placed into you that you are, you will either decide or not to reveal it to all to see. In first it is necessary that you ask to be seeing of this to rise. You are the knower of all that one is to feel if in a requirement of this self to find her way.

You appear lost in this interact as if to not know of your way.....

Let us guide you; to hover beside you, to entice you, to interact with you in a voice that is powerful beyond recognition of it to be yours, but know this that we speak, it is.

In only this to know of it to be yours you will. You are the commander of your domain so to speak but you have the visionary planted deep to receive this that you are asking to hear.

Can I be an interaction with you to hear? Will this help me find ME?

Yes in this we are to offer you are the hearer of all that is spoken, are you not?

You must challenge this previous version, the trickery of the dated mind to be thought of as the villain here that is to overrule any new thoughts or suggestions by this that you be encouraging to hear her as you to speak. In this version of self all in same to be you are to become knowing of an evolvement that is to take place to emerge into a new framework, this framework of realisation into a newer you that has learnt to call to you and to speak and listen to the leader within. You are hesitant to interact, we ask this of you?

Unsure if I will succeed.

You dear one has already succeeded, for it is to get to this place of awareness, recognition, willingness to hear this voice that be yours in ours to speak as only love, that you did. You are this encouragement that you have been built on and enticing oneself to call to self to see. You are willing in this we ask? YES....

I feel many that will not realise of this to be. Can we {I} help them to find their way?

We speak in a loving way as to describe to you this way in which the rules of the universal interpretation of all that is to go your way. It is in this divine knowing of you that you are. One must be accepting of this mission as your own to be, find your way of this you will dear one, be it not of another's path to find or choose for them, for of this it is that you shall not.

In all to choose this they have and are to find their own way in the decided knowing of this to be theirs to experience.

Are we to leave them to fend for themselves?

As if to speak like it is a war that will be fought then yes! all are interpreters of their greatest assets and faults are in this encouragement by us to receive, it is a battle from within that many of you are to fight in this reality of self to be. This war of contention to be loved or not is a smokescreen of drama that is a human existence to live into, for the deeper you dive the harder it is to ignore this love that you will unearth to cherish, for it is in the un-layering, the unfolding, the re-discovering of you, the real you that you will feel to find love in amongst this human physical emotional interact that feels like evidence of war at times to call of it that.

IN love war is won, is it not?

A continual defamation that all humans are privy to it appears is to be ever negligent to the human self to speak, to believe, to allow of love to enter. Or enter too much we say in the form of another to overtake. It is in this waring that you are to be felt as eligible within self to stop this nonsense and allow of this loving being to take flight so that she may soar and spread her wings to explore and to overtake all that appears as not winnable to the human eye to see.

Will all find their way? Or of this love that you speak.

Yes in a certain way as to explain, their version of love that is required by them to perceive. For you see in this to speak of as love, all are different in their learnings or lessons of what it is that this love is to mean to them. Be it a reckless love, a love that hurts, a love worth dying over, a love that intrudes or extrudes to all that one is to see, it may be a love that is complete never to need another to see of it again, it is a love that may spellbound you, one that disrupts you but ultimately it is in a searching of $LOVE$ perse` that you are all craving to find your way into and of.

IN this version that we see {YOU} you all are loved in this entirety that we be. You are filled with decided intention to become of love as you we do complete.

It is the dousing of the human will that one must, to help extinguish this destructive war zone that has become the determiner from within that will stop at nothing to win, to overrule you into a place of contempt and distraught at the thought that you cannot or will not ever find this love as yours.

It is in this to be your way
to know that you will.

Guidelines to finding my way

- ❖ IN this we are to offer, when one can sit in a releasing state of peace and quiet to realise and feel as it is to fill them, sensing to rise from within that they can, then you shall.

- ❖ Be allowing here in this space of release to feel this you, to let all that she is to contemplate, survey, offer or release be truth and reacted to as in a place to care.

- ❖ In kind knowing of this that you are to be a gentle response or approach to the words, tears, feelings, or emotions that you are to feel, hear or see.

- ❖ Feel ravaged, worn, even deserted one will, for the truthful being of love & light that you are in this awareness to begin to know again, will hold of you here to encourage oneself to grow.

- ❖ Reveal unto this self all that she is in need to see, hear, or know

- ❖ Speak to this YOU^ to allow for yourself to be acknowledged and received by you, no need to judge or discredit in all that is revealed by you to observe.

In here it is that you will feel to find thee.

A pathway of intrigue, love and hope to witness by thee, as you in hurt, anger, or disbelief to sadden this as thee, you will meet the version of you that has resisted, ignored, and betrayed you in a willingness to be seen as or of another to be called as your own.

- ❖ Forgive, Forgive & Forgive some more.

In kind and of gentle heart you will speak to this one, this being that you are as a creature of the creator to have loved thus far. She is seeking you out to feel as to find her way. Let her speak timid or unsure she will this I guarantee, hear her voice meek & mild or angry and loud however it shall sound.

- ❖ Spend time in an interaction once more, to remember and recall the real version that you are to be.

- ❖ Revel in her, feel as she nourishes you as you ask her forgiveness, feel as you receive her again as loved.

- ❖ Feel as your heart is to burst open wide, revealing a love so hidden, defeated even not to have been allowed, you are here in this place of grandest reveal. Can you feel her here to admit defeat?

No longer she chooses to hide or lie for it is in here that I am choosing to find me.

My path of allowance is calling to me to stand upon it, this direction that I seeked as felt to never find, lays before me now ready to stand upon.

This is me, finding my way now clearly set out for me.

These guidelines are they relevant for all?

We are to offer these as suggestions to most; to feel their own way into a place of release and non-resist. It is in a dealing with the human that holds you hard at times of self to be dis-allowing of this discovering of this beauty within that will determine the way in which it all shall be revealed to you.

Many if not most are resistant to the reveal we offer, even more so resist and non-wanting of the process to even start. For to begin with a question such as this…

'Who or What AM I' leads one straight to pandoras box, does it not? A box or as to offer a human form of mixed emotions, a dullened void, a space of non-connect, lack of happiness and it is often in this unsureness that the many of you shy away from the asking of this question to be heard, let alone even attempt to be felt as answered.

Why is this question so BIG?

Hear this dear one; in an asking to be felt as to eliminate or discredit all that one is to feel or think to have thought of themselves to be, as in a noticeably big conclusion or realisation that just maybe they are not. **{Not this self to see}.** One then questions; is this how I have lived into my life being interpreted by me and those that I have witnessed as contributors to me. A sudden vision or realisation appears as if to suddenly comprehend.

Is this really how I have chosen to see me?

It becomes a big question from within in the asker that speaks.

When one is in tuned to the real self it may never rise this question for one to ask.

If like the many that we are to witness upon your earthly existence you as in them are searching, striving, disagreeing, and asking to be of this that they are not to be.

Someone else.

If we were to explain it like this, in all including those in us that we be are the becoming of an evolvement or a significance to become. We as in you have chosen many pathways of opportunities to explore, discover and grow and in this to offer it is the many that have appeared upon the earthly path to be felt as an empowerment to undertake, many have fallen shall we say in regard to the realness that you are, the light body that you are, has fallen by the way side as to be no longer seen or even acknowledged as this in you to be grand or of service. It is a common trait that we witness the many of you in human form to investigate and to search furiously into a becoming or being something that you are not. You strive into another human existence to think that if you were to be different, then my life would be better. Do you not?

Are you suggesting that this 'I' that I see is not me?

In a physical version yes to the physical eyes to observe you are as real as the skin upon your shell. But let us interject here into ones thoughts of a moreness to be. In more we have spoken before and to many regarding this subject to be.

MORE.... Is always a realisation or a unsatiable attitude that all living and non-beings are to have held within?

In a human interpretation it becomes of material matters, often greed, moral injustice and hunger to rule are involved and emotional attachments to this more to speak, does it not?

In the evolved beings of love & light, this non-physical essence to be spoken of as us to know; yes we are always enticed by more, but it is an attitude of acceptance by us that we openly and passionately describe as ourselves always in the receiving of. It just IS. We need no description of an offering, matter, hierarchy, or object to be to suggest to us that we are more. Our infinite being of this love held space of realisation that we are, just knows.

So would you suggest that in more there always is?

Yes dear one in this we would offer that in MORE there always IS more available, yet it appears to be one of the hardest envisionments that a human encasement is to attempt. In the finding of self to be clearly and concisely heard and to be the truth speaker to you in this formation that you are, you will hear of only this divine voice of love as yours to always offer you the right way or the correct way in which it is that one must speak to always hear of this that they be always more.

Believing in more, will this help find ME?

To believe in self as always more, is the way home is it not?

Home to your centre, your lighted core, your very being of loving essence that you are to be seen in all this that we be. So, to envision oneself in this place of more to exist within self as a knowing of deepest truth to speak that you are always a contribution to be found in this place of more; **then you shall always be.** To be this bold speaker of LOVE is to entice all in most to you, to be felt as a calling out of you that comes in times of many to suggest to not only self but to all that are to hear this LOVE that you are to know yourself so divinely and lovingly as, you knowingly emit this display of LOVE to be offered as if to be called a show of expression to most that you are this peace & calm, this certainty within, this viewer of only good to see and most importantly know this that you be ever the receiver of always more to be yours to have.

Finding my way, is likened to more! More information needed here please.

If and when one can comprehend the givenness that you are. To feel as if the unsettled human that holds you has left the building and offers no resist to suggest, then in this place of welcomed calm one will find their view to have changed, will they not?

You as human will become more decided in a way as if to speak lovingly to not only yourself but in all that you interact with. It is in this voice of steadiness that you become a saviour or saint to self to feel this healing, this balancing, this calming to be bestowed upon you to feel. It becomes a deep knowing through belief in yourself to trust this that is you again. To feel the difference in human body as to be assured, strong, or willing again and at most eager to try. This challenge that you have embarked upon the many of you in which it appears to be is this searching for the you that just wants to be loved or happy. Is this not to ask?

How can this contribution of LOVING myself be enough to set me free?

You are the entirety of ALL love we offer; and if one can allow of the human mind to step aside as if to not comment or offer to you in this place to be NOW, you will feel a confusion to start as to of what is it that we mean. Let it be spoken of as in this to speak; LOVE is the grandest yet most overly confused subject to speak into.

Our version of LOVE is a place that never needs to be justified, satisfied, or described. It is in this envisionment that we are to be a knowing eternal, intimate version of this greater aspect into all it is that one is to be. To be the evolvers into and overseers of this great love that is to be the seer of ALL that lights up within thee. We suggest to you here that yes in not a physical body to assume we are this enablement or of this ability to always be enticed by this love as ever eternally felt as us to be. **It is in only love that we speak.**

> In the allowing of self to be LOVE,
> than one shall always be.

Will I find this Love that you speak so desirably of when I find me?

Yes in this to answer as a certainty to be.

You are knowing of this love to begin for it is first established from within in the grandness that you be to have been and to have always been you will hold this infinite love within. You are this knowing in human to express this doubt at times that you are not loved or require of someone to love to make you whole or complete.

Do you not?

> In this asking it allows for a sense
> of rejection or incomplete to be
> thought of as yours, does it not?

One must be a committed version of this self to offer LOVE, to be ever the forgiving being of love to self to hear, to know of ones faults but always to express the absolute best of you is to be acknowledged in all that you do. You strive in this human form to please and to comfort to be this for another no matter the cost or dismiss to you that may be. Let oneself turn the page so to speak and start with this YOU that you see.

How will this help me find me?

By becoming the envisionment of all that one is to see as you. This is to heighten your senses of self to be, becoming the asker of this self

What is it that you see?, Do you like of what it is that you see? Does this that I see align with me? Am I certain in this place to suggest or receive that this is mine to be? Am I being kind to myself here as I speak or receive? Can I feel my truths as in this that I observe, speak, or receive?

Some questions to ask this self to suggest.

Let this being of love that you are, be the ever contributor to this that you are. You are found within this love so grand that we speak of it as you. In this to accept you must. It is a big acceptance this we know especially if and of human form to disagree, to have been living into this life of a lie as to suggest that you have not ever felt this love to attest to as yours to accept or know.

YOU will this we know.

Confidence is a trait of yours in spirit, is this correct to offer?

Let us explain, in confidence it is that one will find her true self to be the greatest speaker that one has ever heard to speak. So yes in this confidence it is to be yours to know.

CHAPTER 4

CONFIDENCE

YEP, that is not me.

Not yet but let us speak.

You are the hidden away, the decided not to see that one has chosen to be, are you not? The quiet, the unresolved, the truth denier, the deliberate attempt to fail, the self-sabotaged.

We ask this of you; WHY?

Is it too hard to observe and accept the beauty that lays within thee?

Yes, I agree, **we know you do. We see all of you.**

To be letting of this self be real, one then does come into contact with all that feels as to hold you back or down. Does one not?

It is in this undecided version of you, the one that has put in place a system that does not include you or serve you. The voice that speaks is not yours to trust or even know. This system has been allowed to run on auto pilot if to call it that, or spoken in a voice as of another is where it appears to us that you have accepted this as right and correct.

> Stand up now and speak these words:
>
> .... I have nothing to hide
>
> .... I am willing to hear
>
> .... I am willing to see
>
> .... I am ready
>
> .... I am ME

How did that feel?

> Challenging, unable to commit, hard to speak, not wanted, deliberate not to speak, tried but did not believe, ignorant to speak, non-allowing.

These are all perfectly presented responses this we offer as yours to accept. It is often in this place of denial, fear, or anxiousness to be that many in human are to be non-allowing of this self to speak and even if you do pretend to speak, you do not believe.

Okay then, lessons in confidence please.

You are willing this we see, to address this subject as lacking in thee?

It appears in many this we are to know that in times too many to mention you [in this lacking confidence] self has listened and behaved as another to be. Knowing no different, you have been directed, guided, and offered to be this that you are not nor ever meant to be. You have followed your siblings, parents, family members, loved ones, leaders & rulers and even those that you do not really know. You have tried it appears to become this version of you that they are to see. It takes a strong sensing from within that is to rival this that has been established or instilled in you from seemingly this place of planetary birth to have become. You are the listener, the seer of all that has been offered to you. Implanted beliefs, truths, and aspects of others that you just thought you might need or felt as not able to disagree with.

Let it not be a place of hesitation here for to unravel you will, to feel this feeling of disbelief as this to be true or not will appear, and to feel lost even more in a voice that is to ask; you will but be felt as to be reassured in this opening, this deserving of you, you will soar to the top to become the perched upon yourself to see, to really see this real version of you.

How do i change?

> Dear one of blessed heart we are
> not asking of you to change, for
> in this that we see is you.

You are this establishment that has come this far, to be the receiver of all that you intended to desire to know. It is hard to describe in a human way of which to understand but the ever loving being that you are knows exactly where it is that you now stand and why. To have been your internal guider so to speak as to the achievements in learnings and experiences that one was to achieve. In all that you have felt to have gathered to this self to be. You are the determiner that lays so lovingly within, it is to have been an offering to such in this human to be that you would lose your ability to love of this self and to be dismissive of all that one is to see as grand beauty in herself. It is apparent to offer that this is true and so in many that have entered this human entity to become. It has been a challenging time we offer here to many to speak of themselves as love and in this kind and true way.

How do i change?

To change is to feel as if this one that you are is not worthy, does it not?

Let all intentions to change be laid to rest, for it is in this discovery that you are deep with intent, that you will find this version of self to speak that is not to desire change but to be more of than ever knowing of self to have been. Your voice becomes a power that stands against all that is said in contempt or revolt of this one to believe in as hers to be. To allow for momentum to gather and to become an asker of this self once again to be attached to a belief in you to see as true to you. So dear one we offer this in as not to change, but you will in a way as to suggest, you will become the better version {the one that we first met}, the deliberate believer into all this that you be, are and still is to be.

Change becomes apparent. Does it not?

Yes in sureness it does. To be the confident speaker of self to hear, this you will.

In an allowance of self to be the acceptor of all that feels as to be new in this version to speak you will find no hesitation it appears as to of what is wrong or right, no longer you will judge this self to be correct or not, non-allowing one is to become of not enough, need never of another to guide you to the heart that speaks. Let all intentions from within as to have been ignorant or unhearing of this beautiful soul to speak, it is so perfectly timed in this as an expression of yours to receive, and in this it is that you will.

Change scares me. Reveal scares me. Owning my truth scares me.

Of course it does this one of human life to have begun. TO have been placed into a suggestion of not to be in however it was placed to be. You were the trustor of all that one was to have seen, to be null and void to the love injection that you were meant to be. You have been still of heart and displaced it appears, so in this envisionment of us in self to appear it feels as if to rock your boat and dishevel one it appears. This voice that has been trying to be heard, asking to be allowed to be heard is of what it is that you are concerned with, is it not?

The scare or fright comes out of a realisation into this that you are not? The fright comes out of *'What are all I know to think of me now,'* the scare comes out of to be thinking what now, it takes away your impression of you that has been so heavily laid to have been not really in truth or to even know of this that you have been to say. It is a great unravelling and one that will strip you bare, reveal all secrets that you have held dear, and to disable your minds speaker to be not allowed as yours to suggest as always this that you need to hear.

Am I prepared?

Are you we ask?

To feel of this as to rise then in an answer to offer, yes you are.

We sense in the many of you there in this establishment as to be spoken of as you in there. You are the seer of all that you perceive to be yours to accept or reject, is this not correct?

In many it is to be the chooser that rules to speak, to be ever the agreed to all that appears as not easy or contented to be.

In this way to live upon your human planet many if not most have asked to achieve divine lessons of love, hurt, knowing and not, so in this to explain all lives are to be an interpretation of you to have asked of self to be. To be the believer in all that one is to see, the lessons come thick and fast and a certainty to be. In a believer of to be not, the lessons still come thick and fast and a certainty to be. {re-read that last sentence}

So, we offer this to explain; that in all that you see, think, and speak to say, you will.

Your words in thoughts dear one are to be some of the most powerful contributions that you shall offer to make. Be wise in all that you speak to offer outwardly to this self to think. For it is of words that are to resonate into an ether of real or not to be explained, to be seen by you as in this physical form to interact or interpret it to be. You are the knower of all this that you be, look around and you will surely see. Of what is it that one sees or not? Be allowing here in this place to suggest that you have and are the powerful creator of all this is to be. We suggest this to you to feel your way here as to accept that you are a powerful being of love that is to speak in only a need of self to hear to be. Let go of all that does not need to be uttered for it is not of yours that needs this to be. You are the source from within, god in magnificent to be, the light that is to guide thee to be ever the presenter of all that one is to be, so shine dear one outwardly so intently to be this in a confidence to be, to be ever the explainer to thee in this that you are always loved.

CONFIDENCE = CHANGE

Yes in this establishment it does.
You are the seer of all that one is to be, are you not? To be thought of as good and bad, right, and wrong, not and of.

Be allowing dear one here to accept that you are powerful creators that can and will. In this to speak there is no wrong or right that we see, but to be accepted by you in this that one must be to do. You are the asker from the heavens above to call it a place to suggest where you come from, you have been this enlistment to have shown self to come. You have been the asker of this voice to appear, have you not?

If it to have never been an issue or problem to speak than we congratulate you on this to have been. We offer this to hear; many ask to hear in a time that is responsive within them.

So, it is this defined asking that will rise out of many as to the need to know. This is where your connection to us in us is likely to begin again in self to be asked.

We love of you all dear ones in this place of resist to be the holder of something so grand that one can hardly find words to describe of it to be. We label it as love to become easier to see, in this way as to speak one will find the truth deep inside to reach, to hit a spot that is ready to open and to receive, to be a longing that has guided you here to this very particular spot to be the hearer of you in a voice not recognised or knowing of. Let it flow and in this we know it shall. For this voice once heard will never become unknown to you again. It is to be this voice that is attached and connected into this love that we be always a knowing to you in this as self-confidence to be.

I AM challenged by this life to see, why?

I ask myself, Am I bold enough to be?

In this to respond to as an understanding to be yours. Is it that you in this life have let yourself down unwillingly and even unknowingly? It is in the being not, that you have felt as to be a response from within that has failed you, or you have failed yourself. It is in the many of you to realise that they in this day to arrive at, ones as you in a human thought to approach this from this angle to speak you will feel as if to have failed yourselves.

Why do you ask?

In a desperate bid to be this that you feel as though you are not, you as in the many that arrive to this space to speak you feel deflated and let down by the one and only truth that you are or should recognise in this self to be. `LOVE`. You are this being of love that you are and always were meant to be. So, see not to be disheartened but to be more elated and a sense of recognition to become yours that you have made it here to this exact knowing, this exact space in time to be revealed as yours to be. It is in here that all that one felt as a challenge to be the real me was in actual truth the misguided version of you that you have let yourself be, pushing you, confiding in you, and urging you to dive deeper and allow yourself to see. To be the seer of self out from this lifted veil no longer to hide away. You will shine and stand into this confidence of this self to see {YOU} as the only one that is worth a mention in all that she/he is to see. You are to never stray or be misled it is to have been said by the many that we find speaking to us about this journey that one is upon, but to be an honouring from within this thee that you be to have felt this rising on up of this question to ask....

Who & What Am I, this has led you to here, to be this unfathomable enterprise as in only you to see, to feel this respect that becomes a definite knowing from within you to be the spokesperson to all that you ask to view and to be the ever-continual seer of only this beauty to see? **YOU ARE BOLD ENOUGH;** in this we speak dear one for it is of the boldness in you that was to become an awareness to roar to be heard by you to suggest that just maybe you were not being true to you.

WOW, I did not know that confidence could ever feel like this.

To be felt like a willingness in this self to soar, to grow and behave in a way as to have never thought of herself to be. It is not to notice a change but rather a difference in self in all that she speaks, offers, and explains. It is in this new found confidence that one is that is to lead her to her heart felt space to feel this love no longer as to linger not being able to get in but to be the true offeror to this one that speaks that you truly really are this extravagance to be. In confidence comes bold, certainness, and decided to be, you have been a willing passenger to be spoken of in this way as to have been driving around with another in the driver's seat. In as a fearing of to not take the steering wheel but to let another get you to your destination, which be you. To be not true to you, to not value your own opinion over another as more, to be unheard in a dispute or decision that certainly does involve you, to be as felt like unworthy to speak or to think that you are not to know enough to offer.

Let all this be returned to the outerness, the ethers {we describe of release to be} of all this that we be to be the receiving of this grand love and watch to feel as it is to bask you in a light that you have possibly never felt. To recognise this you, this glorious you as in this version of self to have always been but to know that deep down you always knew. You have opened the gate to let the view be widened and more to always see. Stand upon this path of yours for it has always been, it is just in this time that you see present that you here in this now decided to be YOU.

Confidence is a decision to speak as BELIEF IN SELF, is it not?

Yes it is a determination from within that one has to realise or conclude to make. To ask of this self in this space that they see, am I happy with this one that I see?

A simple answer will be received, either yes or no will suffice.

IN the answer to be yes then you are well underway as to becoming this loved energy of this life-imposed version in a human to be. It is in an honesty that one must remark as to the truth that is to be expelled outwardly by you in a need to be heard by you as yours. You are a truth to speak and in the continual way that one is to remark that they are okay, yet it leaves a darkened shadow upon ones heart or to feel as if to carry a load that is too heavy to continue, then you will know.

It is in this offering that one will see if the YES is true or the NO wins once again.

I want to say YES but feel it to be more truthfully NO!

We respect you in this space to feel this honest voice chiming in. It is in this honest way that one is required to speak, to feel like one can and not be judged or displeased. You are to answer always in an honest offering to voice so that you can begin to trust of you again.

Let oneself be the true intender of this self to be to speak, feel as your words are to flow out of you in an eagerness to have been asked to let go and more importantly recognised and heard. TO feel no inhibitions or disrespect to self, to be no longer needed as if to hide of them away. These secrets that one has kept, this constant nagging to never go, this dullness in sensing of self to be not known in her real way. Let it all appear here in this space unravelled and revealed for you to see. It is not to be of another that needs to interpret this that you speak for they will only coerce you or direct you to change, to question your motive in how and why it is that one feels this unrest within.

Write in this space as an offering to you. To be the composer of all that one is to preview as to be an offering to only you. You are the knower of this deep-down truth that one has asked themselves to sit and connect into. Hear your words as in only this that you are to know as yours in truth.

....
....
....
....
....
....
....
....
....
....
....
....
....
....
....
....

Feeling lost in myself. Should I not ask why?

Yes oh you of broken heart (we suggest this in only a human perception to speak)we speak to thee. Batten down the hatches for there is more to come. You are in this place of grand reveal to be felt as caught in a hurricane, a place of utmost contempt to be the receiver of all that one sees as wrong yet knows it to be right, to be a revealing from within that strips you bare to the bones to see this vision as you in an aspect as to have never been seen before. You will know.

I feel like I am a different person or overtaken by another. Is this how I should feel?

We get asked this often in conversations to speak that in a sensing of self to be different or on another planet or reality it is to be explained by many. Yes it is in a new revealing or un-layering that one feels this version of self to be of another, one that they may have never seen or tuned into before. You start to believe that you are going crazy or are being controlled by another at times. It is in this forms expression of self to speak that you will feel as another is to become the responder from within. It becomes a period of second guessing and disbelief that this could be so. Where and how has this been allowed to happen?

Where is this heading for me? Who is this being or new interpretation of myself?

Be in this place of questioning to rise for in here this space of connect to receive you will feel yourself different or to be in a head space as not the usual way to respond. You are in this stage of evolving out of the drudgery of human resistance to become an acknowledgement of this grand master in oneness that you truly be.

Here it is to relay that a direct asking by this you was made; connection allowed to be a viewing of all this that is to appear as inside. It is in this confident way that one must engage with the higher self, the being that feels to be inside, the one that is different to you to appear as in the old way. Let your self-confidence feel into this connection as something different to be, to be a willing asker of all that one is to see, to know, to receive, and you will.

Confidence brings forth Transformation and Certainty. Does it not?

In ones ability to speak in only a confident way about this one that you be, then it is that you will find a certainty attached to the direction in which it is that you will go. In this new direction to reveal you will feel a transformation beginning to appear, this transformation not in such as to change but to allow for you to preview into all that has appeared before you in past, current, and future presentation as to be able to progress more intuitively inside to hear this conversation in a knowing way as to preview, to observe and to challenge even this old way as if it really is or has been to know you.

Transformation dear ones we speak of this easily and often it is to feel in a human skin like a transformation is to begin but it is already aligned within you to speak this fine about you to feel yourself in a truth to unwrap and reveal.

You will know of this to feel like a transformation about to be revealed but in any change however so small it will feel as though you are to step out of this skin into another, does it not? Many changes combined and in line appearing one after the other are to carry you into another concept of this self to see. To be felt like the expressor of not you to see, it is in this process that much doubting comes along and appears as yours to view. Let down your walls and feel this voice speak in her confident & certain way to know that change is apparent and almost guaranteed.

Be Letting

> In this we ask of you to be.

See oneself in this new space of reconnect, to feel deeper into this version of you and watch in awe at what is to arise. It is spellbinding and mystical to call of it that. It is in this magical way that your connection to the higher self is made. To be felt as to recognise her again in this unique way. She will entice you inward in an even more deliberate way, to cast a spell upon you to offer as to never will her to go away. She becomes present in all that one is to do, to become a voice that appears to domineer all that you do {this is good we say}. Be an avid listener to all that she has to say, for she knows you in every way, encourage her to speak in all that you shall do {she will this we say} be your bold in a transformation to appear in this no uncertain way to spring forth out of you in confidence to speak.

> Confidence opens many doors inwardly

CHAPTER 5

I CAN, I WILL

In this we offer yes you can.

It is to become a responsibility within you to feel flow into you that you will speak this word to oneself. This voice of yours has power, it has certainty, and it has love in all the correct ways to respond into to know. You are the viable version in this entity to speak in this way.

I CAN.

You are knowing of this voice, are you not?

Get to know her/ or him for it is in this that they stand victorious in such to be felt as an assault upon this one that remains in the human form to stand. It is the envisioned from within that must be felt to receive in this essence of a love spoken way to be felt as a calling, a war cry, or an outright roar to scream being heard by you in this absolute place of you in this that you be to ask always to be heard as you in this way.

I can, immensely powerful words to offer, yet at the same time very daunting words to speak, would you not agree?

Let it be spoken of in an even more powerful way as to be spoken as.

I will.

Wow! it appears that spirit is pushing you or guiding you to a voice that offers power in a certainty to speak and to be not lacking a confidence in this self to achieve.

Be not taken aback by this statement to call of it as your own. Try it we say.....

If you feel as if it is to sit well within you to speak. It is never to suggest or be felt guided or convinced into anything in regard to this of what it is that one is to or wants to speak. It must come out of you begging to be heard, no remorse in what is to have been said, and willingly spoken out of this heart that be brave & courageous into all that one feels to display. You are the knower of this grand that lays within, are you not?

For we have spoken so lovingly and often about this, that it seems that she /he is unwilling to go away. It is in this way that we are to feel this response from you to display an eagerness in self to be to say. You are the villain at times in past that has held you in contempt, to be the disagree in all that one is to think or present, it has been the captive of this self that has lost her voice or opinion of self. Be not to fear this new sound that is to escape out of you; one of glee attached in a sound of love, hope and trust to be yours to have found.

I will listen.

We like this response, it is one of certain agreeance and a desire to know.

Let it all be unwound this chaos of you in a place as to be not found or feeling lost in amongst all that is or presumes to be yours not to be. You are the willing version we see, that has escaped the exhortation of human reality, no longer bound by nay-sayers, better than and non-lovers of thee. You are to let down these reigns and watch as the old horse that led you to these, disappears light-hearted and free to be. It is this new version of you that will pick up the reigns and she (meaning you) will grab hold to steady thee, she is willing it appears and of this we are to offer that you will agree, she will ride this mare, untrained she may appear but willing to learn, to be felt as a master straddled in a placement upon ready to take the lead.

I like this offering as to be in control, is this really me though?

Many of you in human mind and voice to speak, balk at or are challenged by these words of power to be calling to self as. Are you not?

Is it not to be called a master, a student eager to learn, a powerhouse of love, an agreeance to be just this within oneself to see? It is in the acceptance by you in this human that you be that many of you struggle to view self in this powerful way, let alone speak to hear yourself described in this way.

We offer more to speak.

The human association to words or regarding the response to a word has let the many of you down it is of this we wish to impress upon thee. You are hindered it seems in many to speak yourself as oh powerful one, master within thee, creator with confidence in deed, trusted friend, lover of self >>>>> the list is expansive, *as are you.*

Let yourself speak these words of fine and just so that you in this one can feel the response to grow and emit out of thee. Remove the attached old thoughts of how it is that you have received a word or better still a person, or object in a description such as this. Has it been an interpretation of one to be felt as to not agree or to feel disgust at someone to be bold and proud in all that they be, even a shallow view of power to express from within?

We ask this of you to try, rewire the brain in thought to think and allow for a new meaning of these words to fit , add yourself to this grand list and title it as

> 'The powerful one IS me.'

Grand expectations?

> Author to speak; it is in this previewing or revealing that I am to feel as to respond, that you have remarkably high expectations of and in this that I am to be, WHY?

> If not to speak of self in this way dear one than who else will?

You are the source of your own power, consideration, light, and love. Yes in this we agree, but much of this topic goes unnoticed even to the limits of to disagree that this could be ever me.

We see many stuck or constrained into a version that is not them, and in this we offer it is not this way that we interpret thee. No one is ever lost, stuck or to blame for it is you in this deciding that you have become. To witness this version of self to be, to step back a little as this journey is to progress further into a discovering of this that one is to be.

> You have called to self with such certainty this as you to be.

The succeeder in all confidence that you are, you are.

Look around you; what is it that you see?

You are the caller to this self in this you must see, so if not now than when would be a perfect place to start to call of self as your very own KING/QUEEN.

Spirit it feels to me that you speak in an immensely powerful way, why?

We are the ever-eternal seers of all that one is to see, to be placed so boldly into this version of ourselves to see, to witness the many that are here to serve not another but in only thee to be. You are the great servants from within, the seekers of this great self to see, so in this we offer it is the voice of love that one is to always speak, to feel this immense desire to arise to be yours ever spoken by you in this love as to be infinitely defined.

You are the holder of this powerful lighted love, and it is in this channel of expression that one will feel to respond, to be the seer or not is up to you. This we know that you are being guided in every way by the eternalness that dwells within you. Let us be this to bestow upon you that you are this in every powerful magnificent way to be spoken of by us for in this it is this sovereign being of always love in the all that we see to believe.

I am impressed, should I not be?

You are entitled to this impression to be yours to receive, as is every living and non-physical being to also be recognising of.

It is in the master creator that you were captured to become, to be a design so significant & unique in this one to appear to be the ever-present lover of this self to see. So, why not start here in this your very present now to speak as this entirety to be.

>Impression is yours alone is it not?
>In ones version to be of what
>is it that you see?
>Are you willing to value this
>you in another way?
>Non-conforming to this of
>another but only in you.
>Many assign a deflated value upon
>this that they be, why we ask?
>Know you are the truly
>## MAGNIFICANT
>that we see.

Look through our eyes dear ones to appreciate thee, this earthly creature desperate to be seen, in only a love that fills you strong into this place of endearment to become. You are all this and more in every way of which it is that we are to view, many glimmers, aspects, and fractures of you we see them all enticingly as yours in a loved way to always be this in you, in us to ever be.

This I will intend.

CHAPTER 6

POWERFUL DECIDER WITHIN.

Deciding to become.

Dear ones in this you already are.

It is with relentless passion to describe it of this to be you in human skin are to undertake the most tedious of tasks to become. To be the follower through, the instigator of all to inquire, to be the driving force that feels to bombard you at times to a certain death to explain as physical life to end. It is in this constant state of indecision or disbelief that many of you sit to exaggerate your times of self not and a non-knowing to be. You are the one that is to be the powerful eliminator as in regard to this that you do not see, represented as in bad & good of this ability to be. In a decision or mind made up to search, to ask, to receive you will, and it is often out of this voice of despair that you do.

Asking often in this we are to hear,

Who am I, where do I begin?

Is it not in asking that one should do?

Yes please do, this we offer to explain, if not to ask dear one than of what is it that you will hear to know. Be relentless in your asking for it is of this that we love to do to be the ever supplier to you in a wisdom of kind to be the offerors of all that one is to be, know and receive. It is in this state of asking that one feels to have given up on all that they have tried, and they will at this point in time try anything right.

Yes we agree, for often and it is spoken of by this one in her words to channel about love and respect in a death to be seen in a physical way that the many that are to realise of death impending than this is of what one shall do. Now it is not to say that you are at the end of your life before you decide to ask, but after it has been tried in many attempts in human will to see, hear, know or be one will subside and retract inward to the inner guide, and it is in this voice of humble request to know it is that one shall.

Releasing my human side, is this advised by you.

This human format that you all hold so intently into and to feel as if to parade it out for all to see in a good or not so good interpretation of it to be made. Is your choosing to be. You are the willing holder of this grand to see, to be the beacon of love and light that dwells within thee to be the pathway to enter this establishment to be. In ones releasing as you call it to be one is asked often to soften the hardened exterior form to be acknowledging yes of this gift of life to be seen as yours but to be just this pleased in all that one is to see.

To be the knower of this gift of life in this physical to be called yours to suggest, then yes acknowledge thee **with an intent to call of it loved.**

But in a moreness to explain; it is in just this form that one places so much emphasis upon and it is to appear to us in many to witness thee that it rules or overtakes your existence in this life to be. Does it not?

Human rules.

You as human are ruled and contorted into a version of self-lack, unseen, and unworthiness to be, to be not the beauty or the richest or the one with most is to debilitate thee. It is in this down and out that many of you are to succumb to the words or a voice of wisdom that lets you feel as if to ask this of us.

> ~ I wish to hear, please allow me.

And dear ones it is often in this place of despair that many of you are to simply allow the stronghold of the human to disappear and ask in a raw, defeated, and broken way as if to offer no resistance but just the true version of you to display.

It is here that we enter and let us provide it is not only the broken or the ones that appear to be nearing the end of human life or needing a reprieve into a life to be revoked that will receive, but it is in all that are to ask to feel this to be us in spirit to reflect the real version of you, the truth that you be, is where we make ourselves known. Whether by the sensing of us to be near, to feel us within your energy, or to see us as a vision of angels, god, guides or loved ones that have departed.

So, in bold it is that we offer that yes we are the gifted it appears to visit with you in this state of dis-ease or unrest and it is here that we meet the real asker in you that you be.

Know this to speak that it is not always in a state of exhaust that is to be told by us that you will feel our intent, or to receive thee. This it is not, but it is in an honest, heartfelt space to ask the rising up out of you to know the true and faithful you, is where and more often than not the real version of us is to be known once again by you.

The mention of human rules, begs me to ask, Are we being ruled by those that we have encouraged or placed in a position of power to become our leaders, providers, guiders to us as life needed.

Many assume this role including thee {you} for it is a planet or dimension of learning, gaining, and teaching that appears before thee. All roles are interpreted by you in a placement of what it is that they or this certain one should be to you. It is in a provisory that you came here to be this or that for another whether it be to learn or to receive, to gain or not, to display or partake it is all a wonderment in this reality to be. You are the ones that have encouraged a version of a human that needs leadership, greed to be witnessed and a lack to feel or display for it is in the many that have felt as to be quietened, shunned or unable to express a freedom from within of who and what it is that they really be.

Then in here it is to offer that a greater understanding is needed here to realise of the earth life as it is interpreted to be, for all entered here with this knowing that it would fail {a love so bold to be told in an allowance of it to be forgotten} you planted yourself deep into a life of leadership and dictator ship whether it be to receive or offer, in this deciding it was to prevail, a life following the crowd, to be mustered along and to then realise that if one was to be a spokesperson of this to not agree to, to require not to be the same or conditioned and conformed like others, then it is often that you are shot down, shooshed, considered to alternative or labelled a voodoo practitioner, or even dis-allowed.

Feel this accomplishment to be yours to speak of as, you are all succeeders here into this lived person to be. It is in the many of you that you have leaned into the emotional world of attachment, love & loss, turmoil & sadness, happiness & joy all these scenarios that provoke emotions to be felt as real to see. So, in this way as if to describe it is to be a plane of learning and receiving that is to be felt here in this reality of this to be thought as yours to live into. The human ruling comes about to be spoken of as this; it is in you this requirement of rules and regulations to have been made present to you, you are the asker or life resource in this to be the asker of.

It may appear to you now in this time that life upon your planet particularly yours is changing, is it not?

I answer this as me, YES

Well, it is a contribution that many have made to this planet, this resource of life to be invested into as human and the earth in a whole to see. It is in the acceptance by you that you have made to live into this presentation that you see, all incredibly unique and different to be. To have bought with you many different qualities and expectations to be. In ones deciding of rules to suit thee, and of this we suggest there are many.

To be in a place of receiving this change as to be apparent in all that one is to see, be and do, is the ability from within to acknowledge this asking that you have received to become ever more present in this self to be. To be a knowing realiser of all intended and to speak with words of love in this search as it was to have become a quest to find the real me.

Change is evident = Powerful Decider within

> We love the connection that
> one is to have made~

IN change =   grows allowance, movement, flexibility, and freedom, does it not?

Dear one, we speak these fine words to be a realisation from within that this is you, to have asked for, to be knowing of the ability that one is to always receive, to be always more, to grow and evolve out of this that be thee. So, an acceptance of change is a requirement needed by thee to express as to always see the more in every-thing, every-one and self to be.

It is this imprinted version of 'I' that lays empowered within, to be the hidden aspect of the divine source in all consciousness to be. In many it lays dormant, and a change of direction or opinion is unable to be seen or even contemplated. So often in this lack of movement, one will feel stagnant and unloved or unwilling to be.

It is in this continual movement that you all are whether it be noticeable to you as human shell or not, but the natural version of you as in the living shell has the innate ability to change, progress and grow to evolve, this we are to surely know. So, in this body's ability to knowingly know that it is capable of this wonderous repair, rejuvenation and recreate it does. Be this one to question in all that she sees, does and is to forever question this ability that lays within thee, this ability to expand, to move and be a continuing version of this experience that we would label as SOURCE.

What if I do not feel this change evident, either earthly, spiritually or human in self to speak?

Do not despair dear one for it is a revelation that is to escape you in this human form in times of non-allowing and often recognised upon the timely asking of it to be received.

In many that contribute in an unknowing way or from a place of lack of awareness to appear to change, know of this it is that we speak; you all are contributors of this life to be complete. In ones awareness or level of connection or interaction to source, spirit or light will be yours, you will this we guarantee. Change is inevitable, it is not always apparent to those that do not seek this offering of us to be, they are hence to say to feel or be observed by you as to not require or have any interest in spirit or the beloved to be theirs to see. Leave it alone, we suggest as we often do, not all are to reach to the stars and beyond as you in this that you do. Many are the contributors to all to be seen as to be dumbed down or unwilling to see, it is in all that they play a part or role so valuable to this that we see.

The Universe speaks:

You would not have been created if the universe did not need you.

Every physical and non- aspect, imprint, version, animal, or human to be all are magnificent contributors to this that we be the mass collective consciousness that IS. It is in this containment that one is to feel an uncertainty to be that they learn all they can or appear to gather unto thee to become an open book shall we say as to the learned that they be, this we acknowledge is a right of certainty that has been written in thee. But it is to never assume that because one does not do this or seek and search as you do to be, that they are not contributing to not only us in ALL but to most importantly themselves in this very learned way.

Letting all be their own powerful decider, to see.

- In contribution it is that many are to make.

- In an essence to display as this that they be.

- We see all in this state of to be, just this exact enticement to be.

- Allowance to decide comes from the holder that you be.

- Powerful contributor this you are to be.

Be always this powerful dictator [that is a word to describe] as a ruler, a king or presence to be felt as your voice of bold in you to speak. It is in this becoming of, that we are witnessing to observe that many in human form are becoming this altered state to call it that where they are to be a realising into this that they are aware of a change or transformation to overcome. It is in this way to speak that a change is apparent to many upon this planet to this date to speak and it is in ones allowing of self to be no longer overruled, exploited, or felt as to comply to a set of standards, rules or beliefs that have been imposed upon you in this just to be. In this we realise that to keep peace it is in love that one must speak, but it is to be an honorary governing set of rules or life intentions to live by. In this it is that many of you are to maintain the safe expression of self to live by and into with a deep response to others to be considerate to, and yet are still always open to suggestions or opportunities it is to be spoken of as to begin viewing this world and its inhabitants as another reason to want to feel this change within.

We offer more.

In this voice of reason to explain; it is to further suggest that the many that are earth bound are here to experience love and learning as an aspect of thyself to be remembered. It is in the many if not the most that are to appear willing to view this earth as a loved state or place to reside and are willing to offer kind and just to all that they appear to acknowledge.

Is this not correct to ask?

In this way of interaction, it then becomes a blessed interaction to feel oneself responding into as to **treat thy neighbour as equal than and as in best as you.**

So, it is this invitation that many of you are to feel as love to flow through you to be interpreted as yours to experience. You are this change or transformation to be feeling and are to become the offerors of this love so grand for all to be found in it.

> In this decision to become your own
> powerful decider lays self-worth,
> ability to believe, just from within and
> acknowledgement of ALL that you be.

CHAPTER 7

LOVING ME

Here I stand for all to see!

This is really ME!

Are you willing brave soul to express these words of love like ME?

Loving Me is a challenging task or request to do.

It is in this deciding to become that you were the epitome of love in all that was/ and is to always be. It was out of this essence pure that you were moulded from, it is in this way to describe of you to be always gods aspect and ever seen as us by us in this version of the complete and in order to be. You have become this human version that is to appear to hold you there upon this earthly plane to become an inspiration to this self again. To be a wanter of this love to be felt to explain is of the greatest journey or lesson that one has come here to obtain. In a remembrance of ALL that one is to be and in this we speak decisively of LOVE to be that it is in this great achievement that one will be enticed to the rulers in this that we be to ever offer this love to thee once more.

In a human expression to be felt it is the heavy overlay of the emotional and physical version of self to be that daunts and doubts this you to receive in an honest and open way. Often being caught up in the human experience that this life is to provide that you in many are to feel gripped by self-doubt, unloved and not willing to believe in you.

It becomes apparent to this self upon closer inspection to view self as and then through the eyes of love that lays ever expressing within you upon your asking and discovery of this to be yours to accept. It is in this inspecting of self that much analysing and interpretation is to begin, thus allowing for a forgiveness and understanding to commence. It is in this way that one must be willing to contemplate to receive all that one is to see or perceive, one must trust of this self and if too not that is okay but be willing we say to journal, express or sight all that one is to be on display. Allow for the opening from within to be a connection, one that you wish to make to be the receiver and asker of all that in this you are to be revealed.

Where do I start? How do I begin?

We are to answer this question to be yours to hear; it is in this task as of to love of self to be that appears to many if not the most that are searching of themselves to be that they will not LOVE thee.

It becomes apparent as the physical child being earthly birthed as you are to develop and grow into a human mind to think, a mind and perception that develops out of this child innocent and always accepting of their own thee. It is in this concept that has been accepted by you as humans to be the imitators or the insinuators and the followers to ask of all that one is to be. It is a coping mechanism that is too run rampant at times in most to be a thought or suggestion by another to live this life by. It is the offerors to you, the descendants, the rulers, parents, rich & famous, actors, social media, family, and friends that have helped entirely to shape you. It takes a rebellious soul to defy the parenting or the ruling that is to be heavily present in your society today. To rule another as unjust or not capable of seeing this real version of you seems unfair we will add, as it is in only their own truth to know in this that they have laid upon you or shared with you.

Many are interpreters of themselves to speak to see and to do so this in turn is relayed directly to you from an early age, an age where it is that most are vulnerable, impressable, and uncertain yet as to of who and what it is that they are to be. Many and in this we are to include you, are to live into a restricted or regimented way to think and pattern to live, for it is not by a non-loving way that they have encompassed you but have learnt only from another and are to carry it through. It is not to expect this young self to know better for usually it is this that you do not know. It becomes an entwining from within that feels an infliction of pain and disagreeance that starts to erupt out of thee.

It becomes apparent for some at an early age, a place where they are often caught in a hesitation of self to be willing to express outwardly or confidently even to know at times of how to express this that they be, to enable oneself to grow and to establish this divine from within thee, to be one that is in wanting to see. You in many are to feel this corrupt at times as annoyance and disrespect to falter upon this path that you are to feel as to intercept, to start to hear this voice that rises up and out and causes a chaos of sorts to begin.

Sounds like you are describing life upon this planet as in all it is for most to live.

In this we are dear ones, and it is in this version of you to have arrived here in this age or state of suggest to see, to hear that you will resonate with most of what it is that you hear here. It is in the allowing yes to accept; not blame all that have been to offer to you this learning, their guidance, these beliefs, and comments along your way, many are easy to manipulate and control and it is in the younger versions that this begins, the parenting role has a lot to be to blame or held responsible for in an essence of this self to be regulated and overseen as by the carers of this in young that you all have been. It is not of an asking that many will or try to determine a new concept or version of self to be realised. And it is in most that have once made this decision to be asking that concern and disrupt is to rise. It is in the becoming of this self to find your feet so to speak, to develop your own style becoming an envisioned self to be.

Our interpretation of self seems to get lost here, does it not?

Often yes it is this to comment that one in human form is struggling with parental upbringing, friend/relations or institutions and religion to be felt as fighting against. It is in this development of you that has been closely monitored and moulded into something that sort of is to resemble you.

But this resemblance that we speak to offer is a stark version of the real you. It is in this moulding and ruling of you that has become a placement upon you of how it is that you are to become restricted, your interaction relies on all this that one has observed, learnt, and been offered. So, to experience you, the real you in this now is more than likely to feel as an indifference to all that you thought and acted into to have known.

> Here an unveiling or stripping bare to reveal is received in an asking to start.

Often in this ability to be your own interpreter does not develop until you are responsive for your own self. It grows yes, then deepens the older that you get and are to leave the parents, carer-givers, or institutions and in the leaving, you to begin to fend on own accord. But it is in these early interactions that have placed you into an unwillingness it appears to most to ask this question often....

Who is it that I be?

Desperation is to be felt, anxiousness and a fear is certain to become for to place oneself in this response to hear the answer to this question that you have asked, is a deliberate test to the determiner of this that you be. Let it be spoken of in this your now that it is to feel as an uncertainty to call it of that and you are to be lacking a confidence it appears to most in the way that you interact with not only self but in others to appear. It is a weakness that many are to feel from a judging position and in an awareness of self to be not right or not normal if to call it of that to be{we suggest here to ask; normal is in all that they be their own, is it not?}

Be willing dear ones in this your time to connect to the deeper innerness that be you, no matter the age, or time of your life, for it appears that it has been undone and is to appear to you that you are in need to hear this question to implode; Am I willing to receive?

Many interact into this being of love that they are as if to be an impression or interpretation of another being closely modelled upon and of behaviours and actions to be if not the very same. This is a conditioning that appears to overrule the most in many that are to not know of the true nature that they be, LOVE & LIGHT as this truest most important impression to be.

Blame is a consequence that is not unusual to offer here to others, is it not?

Blame is easy dear ones. Is it not of this that we in you have witnessed?

In an expression of self to appear lost and not recognised in the true version of this self to see one will seek out many it appears to blame and hold responsible as why this contradiction was to have begun and is still to continue to this day.

In the loving of self to be recognised yes it is to appear as a task of much effort and change to be required but in the closing of the blame mode and to feel as not to hold onto this that another has done is a response out of you that is needed to view so that this loving you process can begin.

In times of past and your previous life too date and lives of regression to have lived, you have carried it appears to us that many are to hold captive in ones thoughts as to of what it is that they have done, spoken or been. It is in this way of which it is that we suggest to all that a process of forgiveness is to be asked, for it is in this process of deep reveal that yes it is not to say that immense hurt, disrupt and anger will not be displayed, but in a continuation of this journey being yours to offer is to progress to find this temple of love, this heart spoken gods space, this sacred blessed light to be yours to acknowledge once again more.

LOVE is the answer for all Woes, Wars, and Wrongs, is it not?

We respond fondly in LOVE for it is to be the contender in all that one is to be, the knower of the way to believe, trust and receive that one is to acknowledge as a rightness to be. So let it be spoken of yes it appears to you as in us it is spoken of as truth that LOVE is the expectation that one craves to see, to be enabling of this envisionment to become yours to accept and partake into as this loving being of earthly form that you are to register from within again into this as just and right in all that one is to assume.

Calling forth this process to begin.

In many times of hesitation, it is that we have been present to the one that has asked of this self to please respond in a different way, please choose to hear self as better than or more loved, asked to be received by this self as whole and complete.

Show me an easier path or way is often an offering that we are to have heard being uttered.

Where shall I begin, or better still how shall I begin?

This bettering of oneself appears to lack enthusiasm does it not?

In an asking of this to be in this way allows for indiscretions into a thought of you to be not. It is in this asking to see self as more or better than, does this not allow for a dismantling from within to be a forming of self to feel as not. It is in this way to speak to self that many of you have fallen prey to non-belief within self to always be more and have been this speaker many times in old conversations that you are to struggle it appears to find a new thought, or direction to follow. It is in this ones voice and this we speak as a certainty to be heard that the voice of love that you are is to have an infinite connection to the heart that speaks in only a god consciousness to be. It is in this voice of heart love connection that one must tune herself/ or himself to hear clearly and in a process to receive as your divine love to be spoken as you.

Many we observe to witness that they are to attract to self those that appear to offer to know the right and correct way of choosing to be this that you should be.

Is this not correct to ask? In a way as to find self or to begin this process of self to love, it is that many of you get caught or entangled into a process or order of as spoken by or given to by another. Yes it is to appear easier to follow the direction, guidelines, or workbook of another to appease this self that is searching, this we agree as an option in most humans to sway towards or adopt as their own prophecy's to live into. This is not nor should it be yours to feel content into. All are offerors or contributors to you and you in turn are to be thought of as this to speak, but one must be determined and directional in mind to speak of this that they be to eliminate the little mind, the ruler mind that holds you hostage it appears into a way as to respond to others to offer or this old version of you in little mind to think.

CHANGE is apparent it appears.

A progression into love is to be
apparent in ones self to appear,
it becomes a divine knowing from
within that one will speak to gain
expertise in this becoming of herself
to be. She will allow for all challenges
to be felt and responded into and
accepted to receive as yours to
evolve into. It is to become apparent
to these that ask that they are no
longer to need to be hassled by
another or to search further into
the righteousness of others to feel
themselves in this LOVE to bloom.

It is in this spiritual or energetic response to this love as yours that is a witnessing that is to unfold from within this being that you be to radiate outwardly for all to see. You feel this flow intentional and directed to all that you see, it feels unknowing at times that you are present within this way of which it is that one directs or displays this love to all. To be part or certain within this change that is becoming apparent not only within the human body to respond but to be in allowance of this to see that all that are in a willingness will receive this LOVE as yours in self to be offered outwardly to thee. Many are to receive this love and it is in this that they are to do now in this time of release as to be thought of by you. Love is a constitution of thoughts to be felt to be an imprisonment of this to dissolve all that one feels as not to be. It is in this seeing of self to be the holder of this key ever so magnificent to release or open thee, then it is in this way that one shall receive their or this love to be. One often it appears to speak; fights this attachment or receivement of love to be theirs to feel as not worthy or to acknowledge the grand within thee, much work and contemplation will subside to make way for a place of acceptance to reveal that this love is truly you.

Change becomes apparent in all that one is to do, whether it be to move, resign or to end/ or lose a love that you thought would be forever. In growth and experience comes change. In change it is that we witness in human to be it is to not always lead to great or grand this we see, but it is to become a recognition from within this that you be to know that all change is destined as yours willed to be, it has been written into this plan that you laid for oneself to see, so to be the acknowledger of the greatest change in you and in this we say to finally love you is where the greatest receiving is to be felt as in this love that be you.

LOVING ME
{authors note}:

In this I will {try my very best}, it gets easier as the days continue to evolve and reveal. It is in this searching that I have sought to be the better me that has led me here. This space of acceptance to see this version of me as all that I need to be. To feel as this imposter {I would call it of this physical self that has ruled or contained me}, is to fade and in this allowing she has done, has revealed the real me, the hidden me that has been asking to be exposed in as a vision of this entitlement to see. I feel this display of eagerness to erupt in as to speak of only me as this bettered version of me to be open to express that this is ME. I feel as to no longer respond/ or react to those that see me as still the same or to even disagree with this that I now display as an overabundance in gratitude & love for me to be conveyed. No longer I sit to please another in hope that they shall like, hear, or receive me, this is not of how I wish to be. It is in this view of me, the one being reflected so finely back from the looking glass for me to view, is the only one that I wish to impress and to know that it is this entirety in you {spirit} that I am to reflect. Love is the encourager from deep within that I have subscribed to and now realise this as my intent upon this earthly plane if not only for just this while, to find this love once more and to speak of it as not only my own but to all that I witness to surround me to be. In my becoming this love, I am to certainly grow, to evolve, and to recognise change to be this grand perfect being of love that holds me. Mesmerised I am in this beauty that I see, to feel this perfection radiating out of me, to immerse myself continually into this vision of inspiration to call of it as my own, this is ME. Real, true, and whole in every way.

I AM LOVED, graciously received.

Imprisonment of love

A calling to another to display love to you or for you will place you into this that you would call a prison of self to see locked in. To place another above and beyond thee to call to them as a higher power or envisionment to see, will lessen thee in all conversations that one has with thy self. It is in this empowering or placement of this other to be felt as more worthy, more knowledgeable, more enlightened or evolved than thee that the confusion begins. In ones placement of another as to be an honouring first rather than this being that you are, is to trap many of you in a way in which to think that they must be served or placed before thee, Is this not correct to ask?

Many are captured by rulers of higher labels and titles to assume themselves to require and are contained into structures of government constitutions, associations offering elite-ness, religion and god honouring to be called houses of prayer to be. It is in this that we do not wish to deny the loving embrace or place of prayer to be called forth out of thee to be a place to share, love and show gratitude to all that you see. But it is in the determining of the ones that are to hover over thee in as to rule you to speak for you or guide you into this belief that you are not of this standard that they be. This is not nor ever as it should be. All are to interpret themselves and all others as their very own saints, gods and honourable to be, to be this voice of insistence to speak in word of only love to be felt by you in this human as to be the entitlement in all to be seen in this honourable way.

An awareness to this sensitive soul that dwells within becomes a common asking in all that find their way here to be asking this self to review....

Do I need you or am I to be enough?

I AM ENOUGH.

CHAPTER 8

I AM ENOUGH

^ We honour this channel in her receiving of this chapter as hard to receive, it is written with a knowing of another to have been to offer all this to explain. It is to throw light on the passing of a human by self to explain. Self-harm to end of one's life is spoken of in an honest and open way in this passage to be received.

Yes dear ones; we honour the ones who speak these words of bold in regard to thee.

Many it appears falter here in this realisation to speak of oneself as enough. It is in enough that we offer you as certain to be. To allow of self to call you as enough, one must be the determiner from within to encourage this human physical form to resist and stand out away from all others that call to you to follow or fall into a regimented line. Unless it is in agreeance to all that you are to do, think, be and receive.

Challenge accepted.

We challenge the many of you in this your now to respond to those that you have chosen as to be your leaders, guiders, intuits and lovers or friends to be.

Ask! >>>>> Are they serving ME?
Am I being REAL with them?

This appears harsh to hear but even harder to speak, for it is of human mind and physical being that you have offered yourself to these that appear or have become a necessity of yours to call as your teachers, guides, rulers, and way-showers to be. Righteous they may seem in themselves to be and in your limited view of self this has led you to this clouded judgment of all that they be.

Speak to this heart that you hold in as a loving request for you to see the truth in all that you hold and see what reveals, be prepared it is this that we say that many will hide their truths and taunts from you to be unseeing in as a truth from you. Many are to drop away or disappear in this act of as to not need of them to hear.

It is in an asking that one must do.

>>>>> Are they serving me in this all that I be?

Now let it be spoken of by us in thee to speak; that it is not their responsibility to offer this to you, it has been your weaknesses from within in this to know that you have not been allowing of self to see you as strong, entitled and centred to be, that you will begin to ask in every opportunity of what is it that I am needing to see.

Is what that appears a positive or negative that you are to observe?

To determine of what appears positive[giving] or negative [depleting] as yours to understand it as yours one will view to assess many different contrasts to view and in this they will determine of their own negative or positives to be.

Let us speak in words that have been spoken of in a power known to thee that in ones judgement upon the positive or negative opens a gateway to be calling it this to be a judgment that one is to place on not only their self but on all others that are to be the dedicated choosers of this that they appear to like or not. It is in ones power to know their beliefs or thoughts as such and to silently live into this to speak to know, that out of this version of self comes an understanding to all others that in their beliefs of positive or negative to them is completely their own. It is not of a judgement that you in human need to impress upon another for your negatives are another's positive to see. So, live into this thought as such that you are the powerful chooser from within that guides you so.

Are you to speak that in anothers weakness lays their power?

In these words to be simply put, YES.

In ones power lays a forgiveness unto this self to view outwardly in an accepting way as to view never of another to be wrong or right but to know that they are the seer in all that they might.

In this power that courses through them is the essence of divinity that speaks to them calling, guiding, and ruling within them. In one to peruse another they must be told that in all that be they are.

To call of them as NOT is not yours to speak.

All in their entirety to be speak as I AM enough.

Dismissal of evil or gloom to doubt

This comes out of a judging self to view as to of what appears right or wrong does it not?

To be the evaluator of another or action to be considered yours to speak of is entirely up to you, but one must be careful in opinion offered as to of whose view is it that one is to portray.

Is it yours to impress upon another of what it is that you witness to see?

In this evil that one is to speak it conjures up witchery, dread, negativity, unexplainable acts of disgrace and the not to be thought of as righteousness, even death, does it not?

We speak these words of condemnation that you are to evoke out of this self in a realisation to speak to all in an attitude of love misplaced. It is in this finery of love that you are to prevail and to receive as an open heart that appears in self as to need not to judge the acts or beliefs of another for it is in them that they will be seen as all that they are to appear to themselves to be.

We are neither evil nor good [for all is simply as it is undefined into this that all be] it is not of a consideration that becomes as a description or calling unto as to need. It is in this defilement that many are to interpret all or others in a sense of them not to be as them.

Being a guided intuitive with love attached and compassion and kind in all to see, one will no longer feel this hesitation to call to us in this place of love abound where it is that one will feel of self to change, yes as a great consideration to flow through and yet a deep desire to overcome this human form to eliminate judgement, ratification not only upon self but all others that are to present to you. It is in this way of reaction or action to another that you in this human façade will feel as to allow for all heavy contradicting comments and thoughts to fall away as to no longer refer back to them or reference them, and it is in this state that you will Bloom.

Self-Harm verses Speaking your I AM

In this subject to classify are your words of offering to you to hear, is it not?

In ones assumption of self to rate, address or feel confused into is where the misconception of the real you lay. It is in this addressing of self in a not so honourable way as if to dismiss and reject all that one has to say. It feels apparent within the many that have not yet felt this voice of consideration or love to rise. It will if intended this we are sure.

> Many journeys are pre-existent and pre-paved and you as the soul expression of self to be entirely love is the holder of what appears to be your secrets sovereignly held within, to feel as if not to know is frankly spoken by human form but one must be allowing of all to unveil.

^ We honour this channel in her receiving of this chapter as hard to receive, it is written with the energy of another to have been to offer all this to explain. It is to explain the passing of a human by self to explain. Self-harm to end of ones life is spoken of frankly in this passage to be received.

When a human life feels as to be not enough, but the spirited soul knows all that is to unfold and be allowed to evolve.

> We in spirit speak this passage of death as it is received.

Life as spoken by one that has returned home; Soul evolvement and review is spoken of here and will be a true offering from an eternal energy who is always complete in this spirited LOVE.

Life impression received; Being human in a constant state as to condemn and displace ones judgement as to always lean away from self as to be right, will continue to defecate this self to the place of self-destruct and mistrust. It becomes a place of deathly thoughts and to feel as not a worthiness to portray or continue into this life as you in human to be. It is a place of deep dark reveal that one will feel this struggle and fight to eliminate all {if any} thoughts that one has towards themselves being willing to try or succeed. It is in this dark domain that you as the human will begin or start a process of

which it is that we would call of to erase,
spiralling downwardly erasing all images of
love in this self to be found or responded
to. One sees only their own will at this
time and in this will it is apparent that they
will not even if they could try, this lack
of support in themselves is to lessen in
each and every day. To deepen this state
is to be an allowance by this physical
form to give up, inability to see self or as
worthy, to feel as unable to respond and
non-willing, and unknowing of how to try.
Feeling ALONE. Feeling UNVALUABLE.

To view of self in this debilitated state,
one of illness, dis-ease, despair, great
sadness, misery, or a hatred of self to
convey, bombarded with embarrassment.
It becomes a battle with this mind of
strength and power that has taken control
of your thoughts of this that you be not.

To lose this vision of self as right and a lust for life to be. Living in a state of regret unable to comprehend of this life to be. The mind becomes confused as do you by the continual interactions that are being offered here to the hearer of all this that is being incorrectly interpreted and said.

One has spoken of this in many reviews and stories of this loss to be offered but it is in this close connection to those that have been in a place of such despair that they leave an impression upon those that are to have been left behind, to offer; 'still to live this life without them to survive.' It is a place of neglect to speak where many are to feel inadequate, deliberate to find peace or rest, the turmoil of the conversations that go on inside their own head is to distract them and drive them to feel no quiet or silence to ever be theirs again. It is to be a place of demeaning power that feels to drive them even deeper into their thoughts that they can and will control this one day, if in a position as such to get away, to survive this torture of non-discrete to speak of themselves in this way. It is a place of such vast non coherent assessment to be a viable source of self to destruct, become unseeable or disappear and in this place yes it is often described as evil, depleting, dark or even to be subject to the non-believing way. It is in this place of unjust and dis-ease that many upon your planet are to sit to feel this negate into all it is that they are and are unable to escape. The many that are to determine themselves as an unwillingness or unworthiness to turn and face the other way, and it is in this struggle that we have been present to witness those of you that have failed [often unable to ask for help and in not knowing of how to make this all go away or end] in a sense of this that you can and could if only one was able to shake off this demon that feels as to never go away. It is a struggle not only daily, but minute by minute, thought by thought as to how it is that you can make it pause or quieten if only just for one pure or real thought to be able to flow in a clear and concise way. To see no future or need to exist, is a place of restriction and containment to be, yet it is also balanced out by the instruct from within that if this were to end, 'I' would find some peace.

It is in the removal of self from upon this planet as to leave this earthly plane behind that the many of you that struggle in this confinement of to see of yourself as no other way. To feel robbed of love, peace, and contentment to be thought of as yours to ever know of or to receive again, many of you will stray upon this path to seek a rest or sentence within to confine you to speak.

It is in this belief that develops from within as demeaning criticism & mistrust formed that you cannot or do not know how to allow of self to be viewed in a glorious way. This is unimaginable [yet very real to explain by those that appear to suffer in this way] and will never be one to be displayed drawing further inward and rejecting the outerness of life is a place you continue to stay. Being pulled further inward (we suggest this inward as a place to hide) and rejecting this self to be of any-thing worthy to be said. It is a constant place of torment, and a threatening ego comes in to play, to be ever enticed by the thought of elimination or even death is a place that drags you to feel as if to consent.

In a place of dread or drudgery to see never any bright or good or to even wish to experience this love for self again is a place of bargaining to begin to suggest to self if only just to stay for another day you will find some peace and satisfy or please all those that are to witness you this way. It becomes a battle of the mind and wits that you are held into to see yourself this way. Your outward view or distorted human version of you becomes a demerited state to see and you stop looking or wishing to see. It is in this state of unexplainable sad and unkept that you exist ever hopeful in words of another that you can and will find some peace. The longing to succeed fades and leaves you weakened until empty to be no longer able to hold the eyes of others that love of you so, and to feel this waring from within to win. In every second of your so now you see no peace to end unless you are not around. The continual fighting that appears to never cease with no end in sight, to never sleep or if to do it is restless and not conducive to you. You are caught in this cycle as it is to describe a hole so dark and deep that only your demons live inside with you. It is in constant inner talk that you try to feel at least to see yourself as to survive, the pressure mounts and you become eager to succeed to end this life as it is empty now for you to see. The vision of love is lost and never or extremely hard to receive and it is not that you have lost faith in life but see no other way around this discontent that eats you up from inside. A darkened unsettling starts to erode you away as to feel lacking and lost, and despair becomes your companion inside your head, relaying to the physical form a lack of love and trust so that you can hardly even depend on this body to carry you along, often being on auto pilot as if to suggest. It is in an observation that is relayed by many that are on the outside of you that you feel their disappointment and lack of trust in you to view of you. You become a darkened state of pretend and or misery within that oozes out of you as much as you try to not show the sad that you hold yourself in. It is in this that many are to reach out to you, encouraging and offering advice, we sit with you to experience this, to react to the needs of others, appears too far out weigh those of yours to get better or to mend and find yourself again. To lessen oneself in thoughts of not to be, leads one down a shaky path of mistrust, hate and dread to see. It empowers you if to use these words from those of us that have been unwilling to be, to feel as if our life has and is slipping through our hold or passing us by. And it is in this empowered state of decision to have been made or at the very least contemplated that one within this human essence feels as if to be in control of something.

We feel as if to not want to be present in this day or life to watch as we slowly fade away. It becomes a quest or drive from within to shake this ghost or darkened state if only we knew how, and it appears in many that have departed this way that they cannot or find it hard to explain, it is to leave behind the sweet loves and life that you have constructed and played yet to feel as if to not love of this life or them any longer to say. To gather enough momentum to see them as in family or loves to become the most important offering to you to stay alive depletes you even more to a place that you cannot even begin to explain. We see the many of you leave this earthly plane, a place of hope and success as to of why it was that you came to be the witnesses of all that you have been and to have experienced in this life to have existed into. It is in a deeper request of success to evolve, to become an internal knowing of that you are not and will feel the need to continue to become, in this described as a leaving or exit is entertained and you will if feel the end to surpass all that you have decided that you cannot contain. It is to leave with an apprehension of this to be of great regret and often to have felt to return to continue if only you had the strength to go on. Regret falls upon your shoulders, in leaving you realise that you cannot succeed in this life to be yours, and then you depart to leave this human energy to rest as you appear again into this loving space (in us) to become acknowledged once again. Always to be received and enwrapped in a loving aspect of god's presence, you will never feel the need of shame or distain for you are the receiver of all that this one became, you are to preview in great depth and detail, this that one cannot and will not ever explain to be the responder, the interactor, and the lover in all this that you are to be.

It is spoken by many as a silent killer or a battle of the mind dis-eased to be thought of and in this offering it is that you will receive that not all that face this reality of despair and unable to repair will feel the need to tragically end this version of physical life to appear but will make a choice to find the strength and offerings from within to succeed and to become again, they will insist in every way that they are to fight of this bodily dis-ease, this unjust so that they will succeed. We see it as not to defame those that have lost their fight with the manic thoughts or a will to live and of self to be unable to see of this love that is forever grand within thee. It is to come as a suggestion to here that they will revisit this fight and achieve in all that they are to require, to receive, to know of themselves in an even bolder way as to offer outwardly that next time they will succeed to be the responder and viewer of this great love to be.

Message received from a loving energy that once lived as a loved human with a family and friends that loved him and were devoted to him, but in this soulful knowing of self he decided that he needed to go.

~In loving memory of my past husband David.

~I am thankful in all that he offers through his eternal being as a love so grand for me to receive.

~Allowing this one to flow in a conversation to express this forms energy as to explain and describe of all that he was and desired to experience in this lifetime.

These writings are to be his expressed through him to offer this interpretation of a human life that is deceased or to have passed in as a physical being to explain.

In ones offering it is to explain this by us in spirit to offer that not all that leave this earthly plane to exist knowingly as love and light once more are to have designed this as theirs to receive, it is a deepening within that drives this human form as if in to not believe in all that one is to be, do, and see.

In many that are experiencing this pain of not enough, or bodily dis-ease even a hatred for all that they assume self to be, in as a human life to exist. These energies are often realising of the souls impress to acknowledge that they can not nor ever will succeed in all that this soul is asking to experience and it appears that to leave is the easy way out we would have been witness to hear, this we offer not as truth to speak. It is of grand and decisive deciding that must be undertaken in another reality or dimension to partake into or even be considerate of this as an option to preview or acknowledge.

In ones envisionment within this souls journey to ask, it becomes a knowing of guided intuition from within that they are not to receive in all that they were to have asked for this souls evolving, this time round. So, you see, if not the path or decision of the human to decide it will be defined as a souls insistence to respond to its own knowing as in this to deliver an end or ceasing of journey.

We offer this in more to receive that often
it is the 'will of human' to experience
as in a strength to defy or negate
the souls justification to continue this
lifetimes learnings as important, that
a human will of power will enable this
departing to succeed or play out.

Lessons in and of human will we offer an
explanation, are to be a prominent insertion
and attribute for human beings in this
essence to have been given, and this is a
reasoning within to experience a version of
self as to be satisfied or not, for in many
a strength described as 'human will' has
become this powerful contributor to many
if not all in this lifetime to experience.

We see this not as a negative attribute
but rather an offering to grow, evolve
and challenge this being in the all
that one is to become again.

The soul we explain is the major contributor it is to speak of it as truth, although we acknowledge the combining of spirited human will to impress as an opportunity to overrule will and takes precedent in this that ones soul would be inclined to display or play out.

A battle of the wills {Soul against Human will} it appears to be, this is a decision of utmost importance and all that is received is honoured, it appears as not to be an understanding of or by many as in an earthly form to receive or acknowledge, but let it be spoken of as this in a souls reviewing of this lifetime to have existed into; it is a grand discovery of lessons, evolving and learnings to receive.

We speak as this to know.

IN lacking from within, does this begin?

> It is to be a hesitation that we
> would feel you to speak to classify
> all that try are to succeed.

It is in this divine knowing that they be, that they are the commander of thee and are in this place of absolute to see to be the informer from within that guides thee. It is a place of quest or desire to be received not in a humanly knowing of the soul to request and in times to receive this to read it is felt as a saddening place to accept that this is a reason for the loved version that you see to end the relationship with you and in all family/ friends and human existence. It is a place of deeper request that will be a response in human to defend to enter into this waring and feud that appears in ones head, it is a determiner of strength that they spar with on a continual basis that you would call day to day. In most it is to succeed and feel the will to live and to gather and acknowledge this as a deep, valuable lesson to learn [here it is to offer that many will spar with this hidden deceit on and off throughout ones physical life] but in return they are to experience a lesson so valuable to carry and this we call self-love and reconnect and value their own love.

Life for the others that succeed into this attempt to depart are often caught in a confusion and commotion of will I or not. They are to debate back and forth weighing up the pros and cons until the pros get harder and harder to see or believe, it is in this empowerment from within this love that they appear to be lost to, that they will admit defeat but not as to blame them or shun them for they have fought and resisted this feeling of not to survive. It becomes a demising within that takes hold to interrupt in all that they do, unable to play or act into this representation that appears of them to be for you. They carry in them this saddened heart that is looking for reprieve and silence, a place to just rest and in this decision it is that one feels heavy with the faults that they have failed the test. It is never to be suggested or spoken of in this way for they have willingly tried and searched for a way out, or a release and it appears to get too dark, too heavy to carry for them to continue and will take what appears to be called the easy way out.

This we deny and in all that are spoken of in here by this one in this way knows of this to receive as the greatest challenge of this life to be, is to be a seer of never yourself to be felt in love than this is to become a magnitudial disembodiment to the human

life to exist into as to begun.
In all if not most that are to cease this experiment or experience in this way are to deal with and comprehend in and of this in the most magnificent way, a soul filled source learning, a way of etherical/light being learning and completion to be or not is to be called forth out of them to receive or preview of this that they be the ever embodiment of love and light to be. They will IN this knowing it is that they will exist in LOVE impressed to be ever the continual version of you and ME it is in this offering that is to be felt here in this now by you that many will feel a release or a new found love to understand that in everyone's journey it is all to be found, this eternal ever given love to be bound into and it is to appear that our souls expression is to far outweigh this human to ever be.

~ In kind it is that we speak these words to offer to this channel in this way as to be felt expressed out of her to interpret this subject this way. In all that be, we are and are to be ever the lovingness that you are to review upon your completion in this human life to be.

In the many that are to succumb or fall victim to this as if to be the prey to this dis-ease this unrest and unjust that falls upon thee, it is in not nor ever a comparison to be made that all are to enter into this contract of life as to have been made. It is in a feeling of deception a wide web of deceit and contempt that fills their own head, it becomes a challenged life, a path that one cannot see their own way ahead and they are to feel depleted and defeated as to not know of how to get ahead or out of this darkened space, to allow or to eliminate these thoughts that cross their way in a thinking of as to end this life that they live. It is in never a haste to be thought that they have concluded that this is the way in which it shall end. In most if not many they have struggled to this the very day that they depart to release, raise, or rally up an emotion, any emotion that is to feel good and them to ask of themselves to believe in this as true, is a challenge that feels to be surreal. It is in this embodiment of self to be since a loving being that the reaction to self is to release that they can if they could find a love for thee. It is in asking that they will have tried to express but often it is left too late to try and combat this war of words that goes round and round inside their head.

Authors personal note:

> It is in this that I wish to relay that I never have felt as to have laid or offered blame towards what has been my personal experience regarding suicide and how/ or why this topic was presented to myself to live into. It has developed into a learning lesson of love and forgiveness to teach me to open my heart so wide and big to let the departed in and to feel of him there so close so that he knows that all is forgiven {as in his sensing to feel as this to be required or asked by him} and that I know of him to be forever near. I feel as not to condemn or assume in their passing or departure or this choosing for self to be made, for the hurt and ache that they express within a spirit connection to establish, is enough to feel this within them that they are to experience this life in another way. A journey far grander and greater than us in human physicality can ever comprehend and it is in this divine knowing that I will always be ever the connected with his messages and energy to be felt, to receive as a soulful connection of LOVE.

I AM ENOUGH cont'd. In Death & Life.

This chapter was to have felt as to disembark onto another version of I AM ENOUGH to explain for it is too often feel an imbalance from within that allows for all to arise, does it not?

IN an explanation to be received by us in this version that speaks, we are the ever instigators of this self to see, to be always in a place of this personality to receive, when one chooses to see thee, in us to be. We are allowing of all that one offers to ask to be felt as obtained in a truth and defined knowing that this is thee.

> You are the establishment that serves thee, are you not?
>
> We ask this question for some it appears not.

In many it is to discover this real you attending your thoughts and conversations disorients thee. In many conversations it is to have had that you will find of self to be lacking in a voice of self-construct and confidence to be, you will feel deflated and unheard it is of this that we have been witness to . In an allowing of all to feel as if to be enough, then this substance from within known as self-love is to over flow and infuse everything in love. This new found love; the love of you that you ask to receive to hear, this valuable asset that we know was placed by you to endear is this version of you that explains that you are always enough in the I AM that you came.

In a continuation to appear to be felt forward moving and of movement in the right direction as in a satisfaction within self to appear it is this realisation that one is to step into as to be felt as a love for self and of nothing to fear. It is often in a realisation that you are to be on the wrong track or feel as if to not be moving in any direction so to speak that this lack or displacement appears within thee.

Guidance to advise; How to know one is on the right path please.

We stand ever deliberate in this that you be for it is to know by now that we are you in all and everything that you are to be. It is in this invisibility that often is to cause distain as to the real you to be a view that you wish to know to see. It is in all possibilities and capabilities that you are here and have become. It is to be spoken of like this in a voice so direct and sure that you are this in everything to become apparent to you to see.

My view is my right path, is this correct to ask?

Well, it is to have been spoken over and over again by many if not most that see it in this way.

> In all that you see you shall be.

This is a powerful quote, but how does it respond to ME?

To view of self in a limited version to be, or of one that is so grandeurs in all that she/ he be, **Is where your image or projection of this life is to be.** In a receiving of self to speak in only right and upbeat it is this that one will feel as if to walk this life along a very agreeable path to feel the inner guidance that you be, is to guide and support you to a place that pleases thee, does it not?

In ones disposition of self to be a life lived as misery, scarcity and unkind to self to allow to see, this disables ones version of this magnificent self to see{ here it is that we wish to interject that many lessons are learned in this way, as to be the receiver of in a grander more soul based way}

You are the brilliance or rejection that you choose to see.

Your path is to feel unencumbered if in allowance of one to be the ever-truthful speaker and receiver of this love to be. It is in a nature of truth to be felt spoken by you in all that one shall entertain that they will feel as if this life is grand in every way. To be in allowance of always LOVE to awash over thee and in a response to always be. It is in this endearing self to speak that you will feel as if life is precisely as you planned it to be.

In a joyous expression you will always receive.

> In this response to be felt evoked out of me I require to see of what it is that I am to be, to be felt as enough I feel as though I need to know more.
>
> More of who and what it is that I am now that I stand on this brink of breakthrough to receive. I am close I feel this to be.

Oh, dear one it is in always this desire for more that this question to ask is to arise. In the more to be felt as in a growth of self and to understand &

discover the thee that you be is always more is it not?

To envision of self as always a receiver or interpreter to have more is this blessed feeling from within that expands and extends your soul to be. In a desire to feel righteous from within in an understanding as to accept of self in this way, to be the realiser of in this that you be you are always of and in a more to see. To feel this expansion that unfolds from within in a suggest to ask or feel as a change to commence it is in this establishment that you be the wise seer and ancient elder to be. You are this spokesperson of self to see and on this one must trust of all that she speaks to see.

Am I to believe more in ME?

We speak this way as in a certainty to be. To be this voice that directs and guides you. It is to be apparent from within the voice that speaks whether it be felt to rise on up out of ones heart or gut or even to be felt as to resonate in a ringing to be truth or not is usually enough to believe you are asking to be answered by you. You are this centering when and if you are asking of it to be your truth, to be so devoted to this that you be and to be in a clear space of certain from within that you believe in you.

I feel as to have been let down by my decisions or judgement in the past, why?

In as to second guess yourself! would this be so?

In ones asking to receive it is to be asked with a whole hearted approach attached to be felt as to already know when upon asking that you are the receiver of all that is right and correct. To speak in a voice that holds you still to never falter or quiver in a sense as to not be you to hear. You are the divine wisdom that fills you complete and in this intuitive way, one must release all indecisions surrounding thoughts of as already been and to allow of self to see this clear runway of yours to appear. From now on in this very moment .....

> 'I decide to listen to me.'

You are the asker are you not?

It is in this straightforward way we present to be to ask.

Can I answer a definite YES, or do I feel to linger or hesitate to suggest NO or unable to agree?

In this we offer if YES appears in a place as to speak with a power attached then you have just answered thee. The answer that appears strong and fast with no remorse attached than this is of what it shall be.

To answer a YES or NO is a determining factor as to of How it is to feel for you, not always a NO is wrong [depending on question asked] it is to feel as strong the response from within that you need.

TRUST YOURSELF MORE

BELIEVING IN ME.

CHAPTER 9

BELIEVING IN ME

'It appears in Ernst of this that we be to be a consolidation from within thee, to feel of this as to rise up and out of thee, to know of this that we believe in you.'

In this loving way we speak of all that in this you are to be. In a deep regard we are for you to be felt as this to rise in you. We have spent many conversations to translate in past to have spoken of to you as to be the *Believer* in oneself to always listen too.

I believe in ME is a sentence that is hard to speak, why?

In many of you as this human to have led yourself into a pool of doubt to be found to be thought of as drowning in a succession of thoughts and conversations, words and attempts to put oneself down. It is often in the voice that resides in your head the little mind that speaks so determinedly to be entrenched into a space to feel as to be the ruler of thee, Is it not?

It is in this voice, this attitude that one holds unto thee to be felt as to not be in a good place to respond.

We are to become a certainness, one of steadiness and encouragement to be felt by you as you, to feel to let go, release of all that serves you not and are of no need to be yours to speak or see. It is in this hardened way that one must retract and repeat to self that they are more worthy to thee than of what it appears being offered to you. In a continual loop it appears that many of human constitution are stuck on a hamster wheel going round and around to never feel the confidence or ability to get off. It is to let yourself down in a conversation or thought that has you feeling stuck or subjected to abuse or ridicule or even in as to disagree and to feel as it does not suit me. I disagree.

In this to arise one must feel never to stand to interact or accept for if it is to disagree with your certainty as if to call of this as your own to agree than you must run {no not that serious} but surely to walk or turn away.

You are the server of you, so in this one must agree that all are to be their own offerors YES, but never to be felt as to impose upon another if they are to not agree.

My beliefs may rock another's boat, is this okay?

Rock away we say, for it is in ones offering outwardly that are to be either rejected, contended, or accepted by those that are to be in direct line of contact to speak. It is not of yours to subdue yourself to fade or lose oneself in an opinion that feels strong within you. But it is in all cases that you are to respect the other as if to view it from their understanding to be felt as strongly as yours in suggestion to be. Are you knowing if you are right or wrong? Be allowing dear one to feel that they are right in all that they be and are to suggest this to thee. Allow of self to be strong and strict into a sensing of this to know and feel to need never to impress upon another as to be right for them to see. It is in this way that you are to believe in all that feels right within you and let it be known by you as to speak that you see of it in another way, but it is okay for them to be right to speak.

Your belief is right for you to know, until it needs you to believe of it in another way.

Your beliefs = Your values

IN ones ownership of all that one is to believe into as a responsibility to call it of that in this that they believe as right and true for them is correct. It is to be ascertained from within this knowing that is yours to feel as a belief system to respond to, does it not?

To hear your voice, your body respond, or your inclination towards or away from an offering is a strong recognition towards a certain knowing that you believe or not.

In ones perception to assume of this that they are for or against is in ones deciding as to whether it resonates with them or not. In an assuming that this that you believe is yours to know is where ones questioning is to arise to begin to ask is this mine or not? For it is this that we are to witness that much imposing upon has led to a system of mistrust and confusion being felt in regard to who and of what it is that one must believe.

How do I know if it is my belief or not?

We ask you this dear one, how does it make you feel?

Do you feel a resonance within this subject, person, or conversation to be had as correct?

The intuitive being of love that you are that has felt as to have deserted the many of you or has been left dormant and unresponsive to you to call of it as your own it appears upon its renewal of to be asked to make a stand. It is in this revisiting of the inner guidance to a belief system to be correct and right from within in a grand entitlement to be yours to respond into makes way for a clearing of the forest shall we say, for you to see through the trees and look out upon all that you perceive. It is to be suggested as to be looking beyond the veil, the hidden, the untruths that have irked you or covered your trail, it becomes an apparentness within you 'that you can and will speak in truth.'

Speak boldly of this we say for your voice has been captured into a reasoning of self to be seen in as a view of another to be heavily congested into an opinion or belief of another, has it not?

In ones ability to decide and regain control of all outer resistances and internal offerings to be felt as whether right or wrong is to become a determining from within as to be spoken of as, Is this mine or not?

Mine or not? How do I know?

Feel your way into this question to ask.

Become the believer of you, the impressed upon by none, no matter the urgency in which it is to be spoke. To feel a calmness and sense of stability and control being offered to you by the structured innerness that we would call your internal being of love, is where all inclinations are to be felt. Is this awareness being called to you to speak of as a truth for you or not? Let your inner guider direct you here to this place of stability and just to know of it as a place that cares. Feel into this awareness we offer; for you in a feeling and intuitive being of love will feel the response that you need to hear. Linger not into another for decision, response, or description to be felt to belong, it becomes a timing process that if left to long you will eliminate the gut, and heart to speak and find selection to become the head or mind to think.

Can you explain the gut, heart, and head minds to think please?

In the continuation of a thought or inclination to be felt to ask to rise, it becomes apparent from within does it not of the answer to be felt revealed in as to be a surprise.

Are you so conditioned to the human mind or brain to respond that you have lost contact or connection to the feelers of love and intuition as to be the truth responders from within?

IN their true desiring of truth and content to be found many will overrule the gut and heart and settle for the head to offer much to confuse. It is in the human way of which it appears to respond that the intuitive being has been silenced to such degree that she/he is never to be recognised or heard from again. Lack of trust has stood hold and barred this one from a freedom to speak.

In a way as to respond we offer this suggestion to be made; allow for oneself to feel a response, link into this body of unjust and non-truth in most to be found as to always skip this important process of listening, feeling, and assessing and assuming of the answer to be found. It is in a process where one must protest or reject the gut or the heart to speak or to know of an answer to be found for it has appeared in many to assume that the thinker mind has always been where the answer is to lay. Has it not?

In many the lack of trust in self as the saying 'misjudgement has been mine to live into' it appears in this sentence a lack of belief in this self is to be.

To wade your way through the mistruths, bad judgements and offerings from others is a long succession of your truths to be found as correct and right. In another's persuasion and power over you in this space of lack of belief in self is to degrade you and place you in a place that lacks respect for this self to have an opinion of their own to believe as legitimate in the hearing of.

So the impressing upon this that you be by another and it is prevalent in this society or day and age as it appears to be, for it is the rulers, leaders and hierarchy that are to feel as if to control the masses and compound oneself into a controllable race or society so as to stamp out individual opinions and beliefs to view of differences that can and will rise to the surface if you are willing to allow self to look outside the box and not follow the herd so to speak.

Believing in oneself, appears conflicting at times to go against the flow.

Confrontation always feels as if to evoke out of the human a response that you are not in line with what it is that another is to offer to you as their values or thoughts on how it is that you or life experience should be. It ruffles the ego we say to speak that one feels to disagree, and it dishevels ones ego as to how could you disagree?

Too view past the obvious, one must be willing to neither disagree or agree but be felt as to hold steady from within and know of what makes them feel correct as theirs to accept or not, does not need to be yours to step into. It is never to insinuate that you/ or they are wrong or right for this is not of how an agreeance will be made, but to presume no judgement upon another's point of view whether it be yours to see as correct or not.

I view this as a gruelling task to do, why?

Do you believe in you? we ask.

Are you worthy of your opinions to be clear & concise for you?

Your greatest power lays in your voice of response that flows out of you whether it is to be heard by another or only for you. The belief in oneself lays disqualified and unjust in most as a response to be felt as a recognition of this self to be to know. In ones allowing of this voice to respond in certain and correctness to be, you will feel this struggle to come out of the shroud of deceit and mistruths into which you have leant. It is as we have offered this voice has been controlled by another or others to have been felt as to be speaking not in a voice or response to feel as if your own. It is in the previewing of your responses or thoughts that one will find a worth in self to be bought to the surface and allowed to explain and receive again.

> In an assuming of this to be an arduous task to do we offer in this it shall be.

Much consideration is to be applied to the responses and conversations that are applied to all interaction whether it be with only you to hear or in life events to appear.

In ones voice one appears to waver to not agree, it does not need to be felt as if to disagree or contend with another but to simply *'honour thy self'* and be able to respond in a voice that you know as yours in truth to respect and hear the power that lays in you.

One of powerful voice we speak in this clarity to be yours to speak.

Be allowing of this voice of contentment be yours to escape from within, to be yours of just and right. To feel as to never condemn or reject but only in a sensing of this self to know the strength in your persuasion of self to never suggest, correct or decide for another. It is to be of your voice to honour and to speak to never feel as if to need impress or feel as another to inflict upon you a voice in theirs as yours to be. You are this power from within that knows all of you, to be the ever provider of this that is a truth in you. You are the holder of this voice ever so grand to be the constitution of self to be spoke to need not another to guide you to a place to suggest as a belief in a thought as not to be yours to think.

It is this spirited believer in you that you are to begin to accept again in this righteous state of agreeance and guarantee that you know you are in yours to hear to know as the speaker in right to be. Let yourself be bold in a presentation of this self to worry not of another to disagree for it does not matter if it is not to see or speak the same, all are achieving and becoming in their own way. It is to rest against this sturdy pillar, this centred version of you, to see this light that shines the truth from within you to be responsive to no other in a thought to suggest for they too will find their pillar of honesty within to stand against. It is in this becoming that one must allow for a freedom from within all who speak as in their own way requiring not to register into it as a thought or expectation to be yours the same. Eliminate this uncertainty to let all out, to be the spokesperson from within that will determine your way. To feel your feet upon this path being led so confidently in all that one is to ask as to which way shall I go and of what is it that I need to know. You will be led dear ones in this we offer to say; to the greatest place of ease and just, correct in every way as your voice of powerful truth to resonate in and out of you.

CHAPTER 10

LET THE JOURNEY BEGIN

In this concept of thought to speak as to offer to self to begin this journey; let it be known that it has, is, and always will be ever continual for you to find your way within.

Why is it that we in human describe life in this way?

It is to be a necessity to describe of self like this to suggest to oneself that one can overcome or start into another project or impression of this self to be seen into or of and this enables the human thinker to feel as if to be in control, does it not?

Often it is to describe of the human being as to be a scavenger that inhabits this planet (in this we mean as not to insult) but to be the fossickers, the gatherers, and the caller to oneself to be a finding into that one can be known as or by another to have, be or do. It is to become an inadequacy that fills the many of you in this state of regret, sadness, or inability to see self as grand that you are to like this suggestion of *'let the journey begin'.*

It is to feel a way to express happiness of joy and if I am to begin a new journey than I shall reinvent myself and have more friends, money, or lovers etc or be happier shall I not.

We ask this of you here in this state of comprehension to receive the knower of you this internal being of love that you are to be the hearer of these words to speak to you in regard to. It is the limited seer of human that the many of you live into to be limited in such a way to express self as grand and bold to be that you often feel defeated, unloved, or unlovable and to not have all that it is that one thinks of self to need to be a succession from within and externally.

Let us offer to you to hear of this that we be the beings of love and light that lives deliberate in this essence of self-expression to be. To be the spokesperson from within that enables thee to the greatest heights of success in a loving way to be felt by you, in this we believe entirely of you.

So, to describe of life to begin would this just really describe that we wish to progress, to grow to evolve into a better version of this self to see, be?

Yes, we offer this to be a perfect selection of words to describe ones journey to be here upon this planet to achieve into or become reminding of, for it is often in the elimination of self to hear self-speak in a way as to express love, and confidence and correct guidance to be that they are to feel lost and unlikely to achieve. It is in this confidence found to be lingering within in a way in which to feel like a push or nudge that encourages you as the receiver of all to be to notice and feel an inclination to sit and receive to peel away the outer human layers and allow of oneself to sit to begin in this process of which the many of you are to call spiritual evolution in which the soul will be revealed.

Would you suggest this to be a benefit to all to begin?

In to offer it to be a beginning then we would suggest it as to be not; for it has been an implanted seed integrated so deeply within this consciousness that you be to always strive into a becoming of always more in all to be. So, insist we suggest that you are and always have, will and are yet to become this more as if to begin for it is a collective understanding of belief that dwells within you in a spirited way as to know of it to mean that you always will.

It is an opening of the human thought process and affliction upon oneself in human nature to impose upon oneself unrealistic images or suggestions to self to be or not> It is in this way that the many of you upon this planet go about your day to see of self as limited and unable to hear and see and choose for self to interact unknowing of or 'NOT' as this grand being of love that you be.

To live like this would encourage craziness to be spoken of as us to be, would it not?

Would you call it craziness or a freedom and freeness that is to encompass you to be in this ability to see the real you, the very essence of love in itself to be spoken out of you to be felt by you as to the truer understanding in this that you are to receive. We speak these words for all to comprehend that in ones ability to just be and to need not to know or receive in as to respond to every conversation, image, meditation session, learning, interaction or asking to become a defining from within as to grasp to know totally then in this way it encourages a freedom from within to wander this planet in this 'life' person to be feeling like they can and will express all that resides in them in a deeper acknowledgment of this that they really truly be.

THIS BE YOU, IN ME, IN US TO BE.

Do you feel deliberate enough
in this self to ask to see?

Are you willing to just receive?

Can you feel yourself to respond
in only this that you be?

More often than not continually it is that we are to hear as a response, No I would not or could not allow this as to be me.

How would I begin to enter this state of receiving to be heard by me?

To describe of it as a state into which it is that one appears to enter is correct in this sensing to arise from within to receive this knowing that you be. For it is often in this state to require to know that there is more to you to see, be or do appearing out of an urgency or a long-time conversation within which you have held. It becomes a yearning or a desire that feels to overwhelm you in this human form as to where should I start to find this journey or search of me to begin. Would this not be correct to ask?

In ones ability of which it is that we would call of it to be your will, this decision that you came here to be the holder of all you think to be a power to be bold and wise to choose, let it be spoken of that this is not true and it is too often diminish the many of you into a sense of false pretence of this that you really be. It becomes a determining factor that allows for one at times it overrules the loved heart that is to be truth to you, and it eliminates the softness that you need to be truly relying on you as the spokesperson of all to self to be. It is to be the strength at times yes we admit that the human component needs to progress and push through extremities that appear before oneself to complete or survive even in circumstances that cannot be denied. But in great proportion it is to become an ego loud in speak that deafens you so, to become a nagger from within that tells you that you cannot. In this deafening way it speaks to you, eliminating the soft voice of love yet spoken in a direction so defined to you upon its revealing to you to hear, that you become caught up in this as to be which way do I go, who do I listen to, in what is it that I need to receive.

POWER vs Compromise

or sense of self to defiantly know.

What do you mean by this statement?

In ones allowing of self to be righteous within their own power of self to be negated to the ego that speaks as to be better, or higher than another it becomes a defining form within that surpasses all others that speak in this way{ but as to be a knowing into and as of why they do?} in ones ability to call to the ego in such as to be referred to as a friend or governor from within that speaks of your power to be felt in a compassionate way to react and review and comprehend all that shall come of your way.

EGO rules in many of this we see, why?

To feel a deep lacking from within as to be more important, or to have more than another to impress upon all who see of them to present to another will feel this ego to be the responder first in all that they be. It will deafen them at times to speak outwardly in regard to all that they have, do and be. Belittling the many that they come in contact with just to prove this to thee that they are to always be heard and acknowledged as better than thee.

In their 'I' the bigger version needs approval in all that they are to see.

WHY does this overtake some and not others?

It becomes a defining from within that one requires of self to be heard, viewed, and accepted by others as to be worthy to present. It is in this becoming that greed and assault in a sensing of the way in which it is that one speaks is to be obnoxious and loud and imposing upon all that they are to interact with to be. To rule and possess is a position of power, ego driven as it appears upon your planet that the many of you are subject to and feel unable to stand against this regime in as to control and that represses you all. It is simply a lesson so embedded into thee to acknowledge the grand in this that they be, to be the ever seekers of this life to satisfy them and to be ever the ruler of themselves inside to be.

One of the biggest lessons that the many of you embark upon here in this life upon this planet to achieve is a worthiness in self to be loved and accepted by you which in turn plays outwardly to call to all others to be your determiners of this self to see first

This we say is not the correct way in which self-esteem is to be found by you.

YOU are the determiner primarily into all it is that one is to see, so by becoming the acknowledger of this to be yours to speak first into all it is that one sees and does it will serve you well.

Be the believer in self first, it is this that you suggest?

If one is to promote themselves in as to say 'become your own advocate and spokesperson' in all that is right for you to say, you will begin to believe in this voice of love again and feel this cherishment of you to live into to become ignorant it is of this word that feels hard to say. For most in this lifetime and the many before this that you have been spoken of as to put others first and let yourself not be the receiver first, have you not? This we know to speak of in this way as to be felt as hard and an intrusion upon self to feel guilty or shameful to think of self as to worry not of another but in only you. And it is in this that we agree to be correct for it is not to serve you or fill you first and if you are to worry over others and worldly events as if I need to be doing or responding to them or that particular event should I not?

In the many interactions that we receive to be pleasantly placed into to receive we are the impression of love that is to be felt firstly by you as you in you, to receive of this place of compassion, consideration, and care then you will feel this to well up from within and take care of you in this world or situation that you feel lost to help or understand. Know of this dear one it is not to ask of you to be ignorant to the worldly crisis and events that cause displease and dis-ease, but it is to be more becoming of you to feel you as this loved being of energy that radiates outwardly to all that are to receive this love that be yours first to emit whether they are aware or not of it to be.

This is how the world in all worlds is meant to be interpreted as LOVE.

Compromise is hard is it not?

When spoken like this, then
yes we would agree.

Compromise dear ones does not have to be felt like to retreat or retract or to feel unable to disagree. It is held in ones heart filled to the brim with love in an essence to overpower all that you see, in an ability to not judge or despise but to be a venom that seeks not to destroy words or thoughts, beliefs of another but to soothe you in a sense of lulling in all that you be correct and right in this that you see as theirs to be theirs and not needed by you. Many are to interact in this way as if to feel better than, more knowledgeable or to have an opinion that far outweighs yours to speak of as worth. Know this dear one in this that you are to hear or observe yes they are warranted in every way to speak their truth to be felt as theirs, whether it be theirs or simply another's to have been passed along or to have heard, this does not matter nor shall it to you.

ASK yourself this question to receive
in a truth to be heard as yours,
does this resonate within me or
even better still does it matter?

^For I know of this strength that resides in
me to be mine of truth, love, and wisdom
that I call upon to answer all queries that
I may ask to receive guidance into.

We really are powerful beings, powerful creators, are we not?

YES, If in only ones belief within oneself to be strong, definite, and trusted to be felt as yours to receive, it does not feel the need to overpower that opinion or comment of another or to boast and parade outwardly in a voice that must be heard. It is never thought of as wrong or right in another or yourself to be thought but known by you as your truth to speak and this is all that one needs to succeed within this loving being that you be.

This voice once found will entice you to call to others this we are sure and have been witness to this to be, but be allowing of this urge or need to heal, help and offer to another be a sense of complete within you to know and be not a requiring from you to speak to all in as a respect to them to know that all that feel as you emit this voice of willing love from you in an attempt to remain quiet and uninterrupted by those that impose to know, that they will feel this passionate strength in an unknowing way as to explain of just what it is that you have that they are yet to know.

You are the receiver in this to give, but in a reserved way from within to speak to those that know and will respond in this certain way as if to approach you to request a conversation to begin, and in those that are still upon this path of self-explanation to be felt to grow, they will enter this loving embrace in a time to be known by them to explain as their own.

I feel to struggle with this passage of words to accept it as to just ignore or sit by and not help or offer outwardly my impression of this love in me that be you to others, WHY?

In this heart that be so bold of love to be spoken in, it is to become a defining from within you in this all that one is to be feeling love so grand to speak, to be felt to sit strongly into ones beliefs of this that they be, to be not to think of as another to sway or knock you down into a response that feels as not yours to be found. It is in this loving way that many of you in human form are to react to this new found love and belief in and of oneself again.

It overpowers you this we say in this human to be felt as if to share and respond outwardly to all others to say; `look what I have to share, look what I have found, can I offer this to you to help you in any way`, 'let me guide your way.' In this we do not mean to disrespect the healers, the sayers, the elders, the holders of divinity and speakers of love in any way but the truth be told in this that you are, you will in every way radiate this love in an unintentional way felt at most to be. But know of this dear one you are the helpers, the door openers, the envisioners, the healers, and the movers of this planet committed into an alignment to become a righteous position of this within you that will feel the revolt from those that do not, and it is in this way that you will be the powerful creator of this love to become a generation out of you.

I AM a holder of something so grand to know, in this way of which it is that you describe me to be. Is this correct to ask?

YES, many of you shun this responsibility that is to rise up out of you to be felt as to be the holder of this so grand and in this it is to describe of it as love 'a love so worthy of you to be the founder of it within thee.' To feel your voice, speak in a language that is love and heart based to be spoke, it will entice the best version of you in you to see. It will fill you content and righteous to know, it will never devalue you in a sensing of this self to be nor will it shun or negate this to be another. You are the shiner of this love and light to be, it is in an opening to become that you will sit and watch as it is to progress inwardly calling to you to enter to become the king or queen that rules within thee, You are this almighty and of this you are to feel proud to know that you have overcome the limited beliefs of many that speak as this almighty to be the christ, the king that you shall never be.

It is in this demising of him to be you in all that you allow of self to see and serve that you have felt witnessing too, know this that you are and always were intended of this christ reveal to be. The god within that honours you in all that you have come to be and will carry with you into this eternity of loved being to become. You are the essence of pure sovereignty, forget this not and always speak proud of this in you to hear, say and do.

This path that is revealing itself to me, what if I do not feel the confidence to stand upon it?

We ask of you this, in what is it that you see that scares or intimidates you? To feel an inability to see of self to stand strong and true into this path that has been lit in only for you to see. It is in this contagious view that many of you struggle into, to be willing to receive this direction of guidance to be felt as yours to receive. It has become a lacking in most that are untrusting or fearful of as to what is it that I will see. Be present into this to be revealed, to ask, to speak of all that you uncover. Rejoice in this de-veiling of oneself to witness as you suffer and dis-entangle oneself from the constraints of a human life to hold you to. It is in this that too many stories have been told to have sat willingly into and accepted as yours to be true. It is this imposter that sits within the thinking head to speak that has captured you and lead you incorrectly, in this becoming again associated to the real you this voice of love in a reason to be spoken of as you that you will feel this inclination to rise up and out of you urging and encouraging you to step fully upon this path that has been lighted for you to merge into. This is your guarantee from within that you are indeed willing to become and remember into all it is that you are meant to be.

I still seek reassurance please.

In a forgiveness it is that we are to speak dear ones for you to receive, for it is in this limited space that the many in human contort are to have arrived in this space of inability to accept that you are this grand being to be. It is often in the misguidance and judgement offered and received that the many of you have listened to stories told and truths that appear to be offered if not than hell shall be found as final destination. Shall it not? In these receiving's and often at such a young and impressionable age that the hardening of the outer shell is to begin. It weakens the senses and dullens the light and be stills the voice that was originally yours to shine. It is in this impression that is boldly imposed upon ones such as you to be felt from another as to be you. Let it be spoken of this attitude in this way, **let lose all responses and yes we agree it appears easier to speak in our voice to hear than to actually succeed into as human to be.**

It is this limitation that silences you and dullens you down to just a minute` version of you, to become the empowered by someone other than you. To speak as if to hear another as your voice of wisdom is not for you to do, if what appears to resonate than it is of this for you. But question we ask of you to respond to the inner core that be you to query and forage deeper within to feel as this that responds to you to speak as yours to know.

~ Reassurance dear ones is only an
inadequacy in you to feel the real
you become the challenger into all
it is that one is to do, be , see and
have. Let yourself ring true in this
voice of love that encompasses you.

So many of us here in earthly form ask to be shown the guided path, why is it so hard to see?

It has become this earthly response
out of self to utter these words
such as hard to be, has it not?

Is it not to express outwardly that in all
that appears hard, it is certain to be?

In ones way as such to respond becomes
the voice of reason does it not?

In many it appears that this search of the
earthly path is to elude the many of you
into a false pretence to think of it to be
a grand or righteous description of self to
be thought of as to have or be something,
would this not be correct to offer?

YES I would answer this in my human way as correct to receive.

Then let us re-evaluate the searching and as to what it is that one is hoping to find, this deep search to a devastation to end is to become a desperate asking or unsatiable quest to find something that is not yours to find.

Your soul we offer the grand version of you is the holder of this key or secret as some would explain to offer, but not to be thought of as to never find for you will in only an allowance by you to accept, receive and be guided by this inner voice that is to love of you so to direct you to this place we would call as heaven on earth to experience in this lifetime that you be.

Your guider within is the holder to all the secrets that you keep so decidedly hidden by this unjust voice of to be not as yours to speak. Let the human disembark to cast off shall we offer, to let the grand master that you BE in spirited form speak to you with intuit knowledge and regal wisdom to show you the way. For in a love to speak you will follow your deepest desires and wishes to succeed you in this way as if to know the loving being that you are to always respond to, to ask of and to know in great detail once more.

IN this one must do.

In many it is that we feel this to be a projection or thoughts to allow for your very own reality to be and it is in this responding to all that you be, see, and do that you allow of self to be.

Often with much contemplation attached it is that plans, goals, and decisions are made and interpreted as yours to be. To be the envisioned of all that one is asking to see. It is in this criticising way that many of you are to feel this heavy constrict and demanded way to be. Acknowledge this now and in and of what is it that you see?

Be real in your response and ask this of self to be,
AM I HAPPY?

To condense it down into this one simple task to ask of yourself to enter into, an allowance of this self to speak in a raw and unbiased honesty to reveal to you in human of what is it that you see NOW.

Can you allow oneself to feel this empowerment to become yours to write this suggestion to you to feel as you?

Feel into this self here and allow all that reveals, for it is in the asking of self to channel thoughts and feelings to paper to appear as a reality or visionary aid to be, this wells up old wounds and major discomfort and a need to retreat to feel as not only unable to write or unwilling to describe this self in this way as is needed by you to be revealed as truth. It is hard to willingly sit in a place such as this, to be in a judging reality of self to be felt, it is, and in this we do not disagree. It debilitates the human form to speak of self in this honest way and is often the versions of you that are hidden or pushed to the back ground never to be heard or acknowledged again that rise and threaten thee.

Why, we hear you to ask?

To speak of truth is hard and even harder is this acknowledgement that must rise out of you as in a forgiveness in kind to be allowing to hear of self-speak in this way about the human response that you be. In a response as to be disposed to, one will feel like a failure, to let of self-down, to feel unworthy and not in a position to even entertain within this self that they can or will be able to review of self in this way. It is a task of contemplation that feels like a hesitation to befall you so that one will balk at this task or certainisation to be felt as you.

Why is it valuable to complete this task? Spirit offers: *{reword this as an ingenious approach to speak to the REAL self-}*

To become an honest speaker to self, one must establish this line of truth from within to be willing to speak as this that you be. You are all knowing of this that you are and are the greatest hider of truths, fears and defecations that lay internal within..

So, to establish this line of truth to hear not only your weaknesses if to view them as this. This we do not. Let it be spoken that all that you are is to further oneself into an acceptance of loving this self. It becomes an uncovering, and this can lead to ones confidence being broken, self to feel non responding and to be felt as not willing to see. You are this revealing, bask in it, wallow in it, rejoice in it, pray in it, receive in it and most importantly hear your truths in it.

I feel as if to not want this truth to appear. It feels as if I am not ready to bare all this that I am.

Dear one it is of this vulnerable state that we love of you so, to be the giver to this self to stand in a state of unclothed to be sensitive and raw to feel defeated yet torn open in a sensing of this self to see the REAL ME. You are to expect of this conditioned humanoid that responds to the controller mind to reject and feel as to not trust of this latest version, the real version of you to call forth out of you this honesty to be revealed. It is in this building this reconnect to the higher essence that you be that will wipe away all old patterning and ego insisted attitudes & beliefs to be no longer required by you.

TO journey appears harder than I thought it would be.

We never spoke of it as easy to be, but in this we are quick to offer that you are the insister of all this that it should be. You are the caller to you to witness and observe to create this very version of you. You are empowered by the controller that has lived within to be spoken of in this way as to meld and merge into this brain, this conversation of old and judgements that have got in your way. You laid them upon your skin to view of self in this way, the belief that you have been carrying we ask; were they really yours to see, be or act upon. Be knowing in this truth to appear dear ones this pathway of illumination to appear one that is to dazzle you so, and to feel like it is to be yours to stand into. It becomes this illumination that you will recognise again as to hold dear, eliminating the wrongs or incorrect as simply a reasoning as to of why it was that you were there, to now arrive here.

> It becomes a calling, a roar if
> to speak to be loud in response
> to this self to be heard.

You are willing? Are you not?

Be brave, courageous, and intended to be for this is your revealing that is to strip you bare and reveal a side that you knew was there but determined not to see. Let yourself be immersed in this love that is you, to feel forgiveness wash over you as needed and asked by you. You are the prominent leader here in this light that we see, there is no other that compares to thee. This is your establishment upon this path revealing to you that you are worthy in every step to put yourself here. Allowing becomes an asking to be made clear. In this we offer we hear of all that one asks to receive and if determined by heart space to back it up as a reality of truth to be spoken in as yours to speak then we will hear you this we guarantee.

Why is it these human life journeys are different in interpretation to be seen?

> Are they? We ask or is it just what
> you assume of self to see.

In one's interpretation there lays a lot of room for improvement or adjustment to be received . It becomes this acknowledging of all that you see simply as presented to you in your power of thought and beliefs or perceptions to be.

It is in Ernst that we are to speak to fill you with this receiving so that you shall know that you are all the greatest interpreters of all that one requires to see. Feel as this vision of self to be the receiver is to grow.

> Where, what and whom is it that
> you assume self to be?
>
> What have you allowed to be
> imprinted upon this self to assume
> or perceive this humanoid to be?
>
> It is all in your doing;
> this you are to know.

We ask you here who is it that you think of self to be?

The answer we require of you to bravely remember to speak is ...... YOU!!!

Your assumption of this your journey or aka 'life' is yours entirely to be, it is a profound interaction into all this that you be. In a willingness to experience, to expand and to evolve you did this encouragingly and planning into all this that you shall become. You are knowing of this from the great spirit within yet are determined to undermine the existence of love and light that you be. Being willingly led by ego, others, and this insistence to be that of another and not yourself to be true that you will discover your path or journey rough to navigate or to receive shall we offer to say.

Persistence in this stance to be of another or just as if not to like this self to feel as though you are lacking and should be over there, for that is where the happiness, the better-ness is to lay is it not? or to impress of another or act or ask for another to love you complete, we know that this is the behaviour, and it is this that you do.

`SPIRITS offering.

Allow of self to revise or rewrite shall we offer as to be the newer version or the hidden voice to become known to you to her to feel and to speak. For it is in this debilitating dismissal of self to be unrecognisable as the shining version, then it is in this unseeing way that you shall interpret your life to be. It is in this getting to know of self again to forgive and embrace this version of you that was once maybe still is the leader that you follow, but know of this that we speak that you will upon entering this temple of doom as it appears to be in this instance to feel as anything other than doom and gloom, that you will turn on the lights and light up the inner temple, the inner rooms and shine into all areas that are hidden and are in need to be seen into for of this dear one is the only way in and the only way that you will feel this grand love that we be in you.

CHAPTER 11

WILLING TO BE

~ One must first be felt in this essence as you to begin.~

And in this we know you were.

We speak in this to express that all that have come forward into this collaboration to belong into as if to call of it home, will feel this to become an establishment from within to speak of as their higher source of self to be speaking to and of. We establish this as a ground base to suggest as to where it is that one was to appear to have started from, in our defining of all that is, it is to elaborate a little more into your divinity and of all that you are apparent in and of. It is in this to review that one must receive to become an asker of more so that they can digest this information as to be knowing of self as grander in every aspect of this self to see and in this we say it far outweighs this human impersonator that you are here to be.

I ask you then, why the earthly form? why not just go straight to the top?

It is in cheek that we receive this question, for it is of this that one is to query the 'I AM' as to be an option? Why not?

It would appear in this way to offer dear one that yes in one's ability to foresee themselves as this grand and let us commend all in this state that do, for it is to become apparent to the many of you that have reached thus far and have grown and expanded into this decided understanding that they are far more than what meets the eye to speak.

Be bold in this to describe of self to be for it will serve you well if unattached to the ego expression of as to be better than another. It is in this humble way to receive that one must, to be extravagant from and of this person in self to speak, see and be, but to be ever attentive in the offering outwardly to others to let one assume that they are never better than another.

I AM WILLING TO BE

In this statement dear one we receive that you have accomplished this life to a satisfaction from within to speak that you are to recognise in this beautifulness that you be, YES and it is to be apparent that you are to hear of this self-speak in a boldness that describes you in only love to be receiving and offering outwardly, YES, you are non-judging of this world that you are to appear in and of, YES, all that comes forward to present to you, you are decided within self-eager to see or at least establish this connection as needed to be, YES. This earthly formation that is you is to establish this sense of directness within a voice that is to never hesitate in any thought or question to make, it is to become this voice of divine to whisper out of your souls request to respond to this that you shall know.

I AM WILLING TO HEAR, THIS I KNOW.

This we congratulate you upon dear one, this ability to finally hear present this voice of love that resides within and is to converse in great detail to the envisionment of all in this one that is to reside and be to take hold of you to know that you are this engager of the one in all to be.

Be pleased in this now to speak this voice that sings out in a request to be heard by you in a powerful way as to speak only your truth as most importance to you, in this we are quick to offer that no others truth is to appear wrong it is just not allowed by you to fall prey to another's suggestions as to of what it is that one is to know. You are to become this diligent being of LOVE and it is in this response that we are to hear that you will and are entering into this state of remorse to speak as if to forgive into all that one has felt as not to achieve.

In this becoming that is you, you are to become devoted intently to this you.

I hear you or this that I be that I am now to respond to, to know as my voice of conviction to speak, and in this it is that I know you are strong and decided to be.

We thank you here dear one for the recognition that you impart upon this page as to the responder from within as being grand, bold and full of love and yes it is in this that we say when you are ready you will hear of all it is in this that we have to say.

To assist those that feel as though their voice is not complying with yours, how or what is it to suggest that they must?

Gather not this information that appears prevalent and outwardly spoken by others that are to interject their knowledge or receiving as to be felt as your own. You are to be guided from within and it is in this strong way as to suggest that the less you listen to another the better your communication with the spirited one in you will reveal and develop for you.

You are the holder of this grand knowledge this we know, and it is to be revealed to you in your intent to be placed into and of you to be the guider from within that will speak these words of love upon your recall into and of all this that you are.

YOU ARE WILLING, ARE YOU NOT?

YES, to hear this voice of spirit in a godly fashion to be spoken of as the correctness that dwells within to call you up and out to stand against all that appear as not to hear this that you speak, delve not into another that hears us in another way, this be true for them we say. You are this entitlement all held within and many if not most will receive of us in their own way, special to you and this very essence of light that you be to receive.

Treasure into this that you be, it has been hard to picture or attempt to be, for often it is to have been offered that of what appears before you to see is not a treasure to see. Let go of this indecision in self to speak and be enabling of this vision of perfection to invade thee. We are the offerors of this always to speak, close your eyes dear one and let your imagination run wild, feel as if to leave this earthly presence and plane soaring outwardly, disembarking from the human form as if to hold you to be, to achieve this accomplishment in all that one is to see.

ARE YOU SUGGESTING IMAGINATION?

YES, let us offer you other options to guide you to this place of envisionment to be. You are willing are you not to express of this self in another way?

YES, we offer to you here to let go of constrict and restrict and see yourself there. To use the aid of imagination or visualisation is correct and easy if one is to care.

Establish this exploration to be yours to sit into to request to ask to see to receive in all this that one can be. The sky we say is not the limit but in many conversations it serves you to suggest that this is correct. Let oneself be limitless and achieve all that one feels as if to express, here you are not bound or cohered by another/ or self as to be or not.

You are this limitless interaction and in this it is that we be, to be the ever-favourable thoughts and inspirations to suggest to oneself to be. You are to let yourself feel this sense of freedom from within to be called forth out of you so that you can feel this integration of love begin.

I CAN BE ABSOLUTELY ANY THING HERE?

YES, be filled with no limitations, always passion, and desire for in this space to connect.

You are all of these.

PRACTISE THIS I MUST.

To feel a sense of release and non- conditioning it is that one will in this place to sit and feel freedom from the human structure that you be. It is here that YES you can and will become all it is that you see to view this self as. Inspiration runs wild here, and it is here that many speak of as to lose the human embodiment and feel to be liberated and transformed.

Transformation is mine, is it not?

We speak often in regard to the transformation or change that feels as to overcome this human version or persona to be felt into. It is a place where it is entirely up to you in your ability to expand, to express and to explore. Be daring we say for you can. Envision this self to be the ultimate being of this to exist and dive deep into this very essence of pure spirit to be felt as yours to imagine.

To transform or change is not to be a recognition as such to be desired{ for it is of this that we speak that you are perfect in all this rightness to be as you are} but it is to become a new placement of thoughts and attitudes, desires, and self-respect to see.

To develop a trust or bond with self again that will come out of this process, leading one towards as to help empower ones attitude with the bonus calming of the human psyche and the body in angst to be. You are the embodiment of all that one is to see here, it is in only you that you will trust to venture further, deeper, and more daring upon each return from this state of bliss to peer into.

BE ALL THAT YOU CAN BE.

The universe says YES always ·······..

It is in this simple statement that is offered and has been repeatedly offered by many that are to be felt called forth to speak of the universe as a constant and ever provider to this self to see.

You are knowing this are you not that all that is asked is always responded to and by in the why and of what it appears that one is asking to receive. Let us offer it is not of the title or subject that is usually the asking of that is to be felt respondent to but the way in which it is asked of by the asker to receive. Let us inform you that in this way to speak as if to really truly trust this voice that you be to speak into as a knower of all that it is that one is to desire will rise to be received.

In a way as to respond we are the ever providers of all that feels prevalent whether it be focused upon as good or bad, to offer a thought to you to feel guided by that in ones heart to speak lays truth, love and compassion it enables this human self to feel the power behind the words of offering and to know that all that is asked is of true intent to be seen.

So, in the disbelief from within that many upon this planet that ask to be felt as to receive are often the askers from a state of non-belief and a place of not worthy to receive. It is a powerful desire from within many that we are to observe this asking to arise out of a space of hesitation and timidness to speak into as if and when it will be a viable interaction or observation to be witness to.

In this we offer that all that is asked is offered.

WE say this in every interaction to be spoken of in this way for one must be willing it appears to present outwardly to the all that is to be felt as if to deliver it to you.

YOU are knowing of this power of speech. Are you not?

It dwells in a hesitation to be heard by you as to call it your own power of speech to reside into you. And it is to struggle to come forth to be heard in spoken issue for a doubt or non-trust within this self to be relayed into. You are willing we ask this of you, to hear this divine being of love to speak in a voice that encourages and loves in kind and gentle respect of you to be. TO let her voice of encouragement speak and fill you in this entirety to be called as your voice of powerfulness to become accustomed to hearing.

BE WILLING, we say in this way as to comprehend this deliberate being of love and light that you be to express to you these words that hold such power, either to eliminate or elevate this impression or perception of self to see.

YOU are this bold in voice to speak become conscious again to this interaction whether it be in a guided internally way to speak to self to recognise of the insistent being of love that you be, or whether it be outwardly to suggest to self in always that this be you in a loved way.

Expression to speak is a willingness that must always be a mastering to become yours to evolve outwardly into this presence of self to see. It establishes this imprinted version of you being the I in god to speak within thus enabling a direct line of contact to once again this very being of love and light that you are to correspond into and of.

You are this voice of god it is this that we speak and in it to be unrealising as yet the many of you will fall prey to the conditions and disagreeance that feels as to come your way whether in own doing or another's.

BE EVER WILLING,

we offer this to speak.

Are you suggesting that I AM to change how it is that I speak?

We offer this information to ones such as you to ask that all is okay if it is right and correct with you, is it not?

Let this being of human that speaks so frankly for you at times to suggest that you are incorrect or not of, to be readvised into a corrective state of which to recognise that it is you that you are to prize above all others the most. This enabling the speaker that you are to be open to a change of variance to speak of as a willingness to express change.

It is the constant chitter chatter that many of you are to hold daily, hourly continually into this head of yours to be human dread at times, to be never or unable to hear a correction to self to speak or even better still to be able to quieten this insistent mind that speaks over or against this that you be absolutely loved.

I have always spoken this way, why should I change now?

We ask you this dear one; Is it this voice of love that you respond to in every way or is it a voice that knows no other way as to respond or contribute?

We believe in many to have been witnessed to an expression to be called as thee, that the many of you have outlived this voice to speak as if in to offer that you can see no difference or know of no other way to speak. It has guided you or become of you has it not? This voice that speaks has laid heavy within you and has become unseeing or recognising it is as if to be on autopilot with no assessment of self to be felt as warranted.

This we allow for it is often self-imposed and suggested to by another and in this hesitation to look upon this form and in all that one has to speak; no change will feel needed or apparent to suggest.

Many are held into this remorseful way in which to engage with self and others to be felt as to express in all this

that they feel free to do so. If in ones
assessment of self to be happy and joyful
in a satisfaction that they are to converse
with self and others in an encouraging
and non-judgemental way as if to bestow
love upon all that they are to be present
to, then this we say you are to stay this
way. It serves you well does it not?

But if you are to disregard oneself and
all others as if to be unwilling to see
another's opinion as theirs to speak,
or unable to accept intuitive voice as
your inner king, feel criticism as easy
to offer but not accept in a truthful
way to accept as if needed or not than
one would call this voice harsh at times,
one that sits upon its throne or head
of body to be spoke, it is in this way
that you are to anger quickly or dispute
all others as wrong to be, to be felt
as unkind and unjust in all that you
speak, {often it is this that we offer
that many are unable to see this version
of themselves and will not feel this need
to change}, let this rise for it surely
will in a time to be called their now in
which it is to respond to a voice that
loves and speaks in only kind to know.

I fear in some that their voice has a mind all of its own.

In an offering to speak yes it does appear this way for it has been allowed to speak this way with no need to reassess or self-judge in as a way to be felt as kind. It is often in this voice that appears before you that has been a need to be heard, or a victim in sense of this self to suggest, to have been taught no other way as in never to be spoken to in a kind fashion or loving way. It is this imprint that lays heavy within many; that love has never been accepted or felt as to be received or worthy of. It has been offered and stolen it appears to many that are to speak this way, the lack of trust for others upon your planet have left them harmed and bitter as in a way to respond to not only self but all others. It is a voice yes that often responds in a harsh and fearful way, but forgiveness is required here to sense this loss of love in an innocence of self to be felt as to react. It is in this that many have allowed others to speak for them or have offered them no space to speak as in their own way, so many have overturned the rules of love and compassion and now live into this statement of   'one for all and get out of my way, I know best, and you do not'.

This energy intimidates me, WHY?

To be witnessing of another that speaks without reference to self as love or ever to be felt as loved, is hard to hear is it not? And it is often this elimination from within this self that speaks so out of tune to be felt as harsh and disrespecting of not only themselves but to all others that may pass. It is intriguing this voice to witness for often one is able to hear it calling out to be loved, seen, or heard, is it not?

This we offer let all that appear to be this way to know of the unjust that they are to fight internally within which in turn then portrays outwardly in this statement to suggest,

> `In all I speak to say, I see.'

It is not to feel lack of love for this one that appears very present in this space for you to observe to witness this injustice being served by this that they be in this humanoid to suggest they are and in this way is to be felt a lesson of love in this greatest way to become acknowledged in their own time to see.

It appears hard to change ones voice if unwilling to see.

> In a way to speak it as this, it shall be.

We offer this to you to receive, be always willing in this entirety that you be to be always in a place of willingness to see all as in their own right to be, to be the masters of this incredible journey as their own to see. You are the viewer in this state of them to be felt as a reminder to the deepest depths of you that in turn lays your lighted love to respond out of thee, that you offer this love encouragingly by your heart to speak and to feel as if to shine it outwardly for all that are in time to feel. Need never to adopt a thought to change one in this space to be, for you will not, in only to feel a hinderance from within you to be unable to and then to seek to succeed, this you must not.

> You will not succeed ever to change another. It must come forth out of themself to be.

Be ever the willing to always view you this way, as to accept in all that one is to see as their very decided way as to respond into all it is that they are to be, in this way you will love and feel encouraged from within to speak to only call it as self-love yet to be discovered.

It hurts me so to witness this interaction and feel at a loss to engage in this way to speak.

We have spoken of this in many interactions to have been yours to hear, it is in never another that one must give their power over to them. Let it fall on deafened ears and closed image to see. Be willing to stand into your correct, this light that serves you full and always in love to speak. It is not to be felt as to stand into a direct line of abuse or blatant lie or untruth to express, for it is not of this that we ask you to do. You stand into this effective voice that be yours this knowing of love from within that will guide you to suggest to turn the other cheek, to not engage and to never accept or take it upon oneself to interject, let this version of human be caught in this place as if to be misunderstood in all that they feel to repeat or offer and keep yourself guarded in this presence of love to offer whether outwardly spoken or just to intend. Grow in to this space to recognise that they are on this valuable journey; this placement within themselves to be respondent to and you my dear be willing to serve you as in to walk away. Let oneself never be caught in a circumstance that does not serve you to be the absolute best that you can and feel as if not the need to respond for of this it is often a place that one cannot and will not succeed to stand.

Are you stating that I should never try to help or persuade?

We say this to speak that in all interactions you will feel this human that you be, to be coming from a place of love or not, is this not correct? And in this driven impression that lays within; you will feel a voice of love to overtake you to comply with the Laws of Love spoke to be offered to you, this will enable you to view of all that will benefit and all that will not. Speak into your truth if must; but be willing to silence this vision that you are to entrust as truth to you, to let all be previewers in an honesty of themselves to be.

It is in this helping way that many upon your planet are to play into as to be able to suggest to another a better way, is it not?

It is this nature that is offered outwardly often in haste and disrespect of the other to see as to disregard their own judgement of thee.

You are to know your powerful truth are you not?

Then why would it not to be to ask you this; how is it that you cannot see this powerful truth as their own to be felt, to honour within them in turn to see?

All are believers in their own right to be, so let them serve this honouring from within to be this enablement to become more, to grow and to expand always envisioned in this aspect of self to see.

I desire to help.

> In many we recognise this attribute
> as a response in kind and love.

Lend a helping hand; this is a constitution of love is it not, be accepting though of refusal or rejection for of this it is that most will return as an expression to you. In need becomes a lesson often that one is to find their own way through to see into another version of self to be valuable and an expression to feel as if the need to change rise.

In all that inhabit this earthly plane many are kind hearted and giving and it is to remain this way, for it entitles you to express love and gracious kind heart to all that you feel impressed upon you. This is to feel the flow of love through you that has enabled your heart to expand and feel love to receive and offer, it is often though it appears that many do not feel to speak as you do. In ones allowing for generosity to extend to be seen as never deliberate or noted by others to commend or from a place of recognition to need, let it be as natural as nature to surround you to see. It comes out of a person to feel this to flow, to feel this that they are prosperous in love to show and will ever be the fountain of love to be bestowed.

> Oh, one of gracious heart we love of you so, but in this we also offer we love of all to be so.

It is a character trait or image that one is accepting of self to be seen, let it be recognised within you to see it in all that you in others are to be.

Is this a self-help guide to offer?

If one is to feel as though help with this topic is needed to achieve a love impressed version of self to see, then YES it would appear as a self-help influence to be.

To feel supported in as to suggest to accept that one is requiring of help in regard to this subject to be called...... 'BE WILLING'

Then in this allowance one must feel into a space to receive that they will know in all it is that they feel lacking will be felt received by them in a truthful, honest, and knowing way asked to receive.

IN ones suggestion to self to feel as to ask for help, in this we are to question, help into what?

Be this divine knowing into all it is that you are the holder, the encompassed into the revealing of love in its righteous place of request to be felt by you as yours to respond.

> IN all it is to become known into
> and of what they desire to know.

LOVE = SELF HELP

> We would reword it to be SELF HELP = LOVE, then to add LOVE ONESELF.
>
> It is in this dear ones that we are to express that in ones searching to find oneself and receive a helping hand to be thought of as love, there is much

information out there we are to admit to be sourced through. Let it be spoken of here in kind and just that when one is to follow a path of true reveal from within this being that you are, to be willing to sit into a place of accept and deny to be felt receiving of in all willingness to express this that you be, in all encompassments of oneself to see.

BE REAL HERE, WE ASK THIS SELF TO SEE.

YOU are this envisionment of the real you are you not? one must attach an attitude to this divine intervention that feels to rise on up out of you in this to ask WHO or WHAT AM I? commonly suggested as to find oneself.

Many that we are to respond to in this voice of compassion and guidance to be heard by yours as your own voice of truth, will find oneself enabling of this unravelling, this awareness, this disrobing to begin to be felt as to really get down to the nitty gritty of who and what it is that you are, or more honestly put, really are. Reveal away.

YOU are all that you are to see, are you not?

In this statement which we offer often is to be found your truth.

Hear as you speak to self and others, feel as you respond to questions that rise out of you regarding choice and decision, are you honest in this self to speak, is it your opinion or thought to hear or suggest, does this belief serve you, do you feel in charge of all that you appear, does one love this self-dear? We have lots to offer to question this self with and in this it becomes a sourcing from within to find this voice to speak, dig deep we offer, and it is to be felt like this as an operation to begin, for one must start being honest and truthful to this one that asks···.

YOU as in the many that we contribute into feel this welling up from within to desire this real self to see, often coming to a realisation that they do not even know the real ME. It is in many dear ones that we sit to hear these words of lost and lack to be heard, it becomes a calling out or a voice of request by you to be heard to respond into. It is a place of dampened desire and dread at times to be felt as to look deeply in to see the real you. Can she/he even be recognised any longer or even worse to be seen at all.

This you are to ask, what if I do not recognise her or worse still not like of who and what it is that I reveal.

Feeling work required

YOU are this impression this image, this personality, this player to have become. Feeling as if to respond to oneself and all in a way as to serve them better than oneself. To feel lost into a response as to even recognise it as to be known by you as the real you, where is it that she/he went, when did I decide to let her go or to not require of her/ him anymore.

It feels like this is to become a major unfolding or revealing from within this place of request to see yourself as who it is that you are truly meant to be/ let us suggest it is in this that you be.

STOP & take a peek, it is this one that looks back out at you.

You are never to respond to this self in
such a way as to suggest that you are not
you, this we offer you are and always were.

It is just that many of you have got
lost upon this pathway of intent to
be another, better than, or unable to
call to you to suggest that you can.

You have been manipulated by this
boss {HUMAN YOU} that rules and others
to felt as to have let them command
you. It is in this that we are to speak
of truth that you are this enablement
to have let all this to be felt and
previewed and lived into by you. For in
this achievement that we see into this
that you be, you were the warranted asker
in a sensing of this self to see. Your
pathway of obstruction has led you it
appears not directly to this revelation
as to be you, but it surely has gained
momentum and coerced you no doubtedly to
this place of reveal that you are now to
observe as in this offering to see.

It feels to respond to this asking or reply
in a roundabout way, but in this one must
receive; `that you are in all that you have
tried, loved, and strived. THIS IS YOU.

How did I get here? I feel confused.

Out of this decided knowing to become that you are to reveal oneself ignited from in this ALL to be, you became and in this divine being that you are you revelled into all it is that one was to become again.

So, you see this vision that we would call you to be, listened strongly to her/his intent from within being dragged at times it appears by the will that you came here to possess. Utilising this power of will to be the commander and chief to be disallowing of the intuit being to speak loudly enough at times to guide you more easily. It is in all knowing that you arrived at exactly where it is that you are to be.

MY WHO or WHAT, is NOW?

YES, all that arrive to this point in time or otherwise referred to as your current NOW and will often be in this place of receivership to know that they are MORE than this human to be. This desire to be, embedded within has led you here with not a doubt to be felt by you to know that you are to have arrived. To stand here at the base of a mountain {grand, impressive, and magnificent, solid and strength centred to be}, to express to feel this gathering of many that have succeeded you to become at one with this all that be. We are this suggestion of love that impresses to well up inside, to find this place of recognition in ALL that is you to be. You are this intuit that has gained, sourced, received, deliberated, and strived to succeed.

Welcome we offer to you in this place that you appear to be knowing as to be your NOW.

WHAT NOW?

CHAPTER 12

NOW WHAT?

Welcome to this beautiful version in this vision that we would call it to be YOU

You have travelled so far it appears to arrive to this space to receive, to ask, & to know

Are you willing to be this grand masterpiece to see?

I could get used to this description as ME to be.

This we suggest that you do, to feel this uniqueness that is exclusively yours to respond into, to accept and recognise this liberated being of love that you be, as yours to always be willing to call of oneself to be.

I ask, revealing this new ME, appears harder to do than I imagined, WHY?

When one appears to this version of self to have been entangled into an old stuck and disregarded version to have been, this liberation from within is to feel like one has been dragged through the dirt or muck does it not?

For it is in this way that many of you describe this disrobing to recognise the REAL ME, is to feel like a major upheaval that has happened causing much despair, grief and upset in a way as to rival the old YOU to be put into a place of as to respect, forgive and review that you are now knowing of this to be the 'NEW ME'.

GUIDANCE PLEASE, IN WHAT TO DO.

You are this sanctuary to be found within, to feel oneself step into this oasis, this space of quiet content, being felt as to have won a waring and rivalry that has been battled out inwardly and externally for years. YOU asked many times it feels to suggest, but never receiving the advice that you required or felt still unable to hear, or to see.

YOU are NOW, here in this place to speak of it as a god like state to be spoken of as to hear gods voice of love in all that one is to speak, to be reminded that you are this descriptive version of self to see as your martyr, your servant, your saviour, your goddess to be.

> YOU have arrived at this state of balance & peace, have you not?

Balanced and centred, strong and peace induced feels surreal I offer to speak.

It is in this contribution that many are to feel as to be unworthy or unsure to suggest that this is theirs to acknowledge. Having been entrenched in a human placement of dislike, lack of self-love and distrust in most for many times to speak, it feels as an untruth or non-reality to accept as theirs to be, what if they are to wake up from this dream like state and it all disappears or even worse reverts back to the one that was? Or more importantly, what if it is this dreamlike state that you are waking up out of, we wish to ask?

Stand strong in this envisionment that you see, be willing we offer to suggest to self no other way to see. You are this being of love to have discovered, to have unveiled and revealed in all it is that you are to see. YOU in REAL.

CHAPTER 13

MASTERING THY SELF

I AM the **MASTER** of thy self to see
In this realisation I sit to receive
Instructed from within to be
Ever expressive in voice to speak
Strong to reside into this lighted being
Acknowledged in this absolute to see **ME**
Master creator of this my **LIFE** to be
Essence of spirit to speak
Loved in this being of eternalness as **ME**
Divine expression to radiate
Embrace this **ALL** that **I AM**
Ever wise to wisdom in truth to receive
IN this **LOVE**
I AM MASTER.

Disciplined from within one must BE, to be this impression of this self to see, willing to BE this master of self to be the informant of this grand LOVE to receive.

Sit into this expression of self that has risen to the surface to be faced with an acknowledgement into this one to sense in self to see.

You are this master to desire, this recognition to call forth to be this envisionment of LOVE in all that one sees, speaks & believes self to be.

Established lovingly within in a birthing right to express it as to have become this version of you.

You are this exact to accept in a bold recognition in this perfection of self to see.

Willing in all aspects of this one to BE.

I AM inspired by this one that spirit is to speak of as ME.

Be inspired to be felt beloved one, for you are this inspiration that is you to believe of self to be. It is in this inspiration that you strived to become, to be this encouragement to speak to self in this loving way as if to be your willing encourager in a respect and recognition of this divine being of love and light that you are.

This established voice of yours is to ring true, to sound outwardly, being a resonance from within into this that you are to observe you as this original note of self-expression to speak.

IN ones manifestation of this loving being to have been imploded into, one will acknowledge this LOVE in grand to be felt as yours to respond into in all it is that she/he is to exist into.

Inspiration with a capital 'I'

This inspires ME dear ones to express in this suggestion of ME to be ever the receiver of this love to ask and to always envision this self to be.

Magnificent it is that you in spirit speak of us in this human entity to be calling ourselves, it is in this wording that one is to feel empowered and in love again with this being of always $Love$ and $Light$. It is in this NOW to discover that you have grown, expanded and most importantly remembered this $LOVE$ that is you in grand to be always.

To feel this inspiration as self to recall, to remember and to request this knowledge, this unveiling, this divine knowing to be felt as truth to rise on up out of you in a human to express and to feel freedom to do so. This becomes an enabler to be willing to override this commander that has left one to speak of as uninspired and unwilling to be heard to speak to see. It is in this divine intervention that one is of human consistency would call the impression of spirit to reach into again as to be this becoming of yours to call it of that to be.

Mastering myself, I accept this calling.

In ones assuming of this to be felt as a calling then in this we shall respond. It is to become apparent to the asker that in all that one is to speak of as to feel as to master than they shall. It is in this asking that one will feel this connection to thy self to ask of what is to feel lacking and what is there to feel needed and what is it there to feel requested, and what is there to feel forgiven. It becomes this mastering of self this human self-included that one becomes the asker of all that appears and is to call forth to oneself to access or view into accessed. It is in this divine inspection to call it this, that one will be open to all that appears and will feel a presence of intention from within to speak to all that is to rise. It is in a place of non-judgement that one will choose to sit and feel as if to need not compete or criticise but to be in this opened state of acknowledgement and an awareness of all that one is IS only to be perceived by you.

Speaking to myself.

To feel this voice in its rightness to speak one will be the guidance to self to access. It will appear apparent to this human to be that you will establish this relationship again to source, love and lightedness from within, to be felt interjected into all it is that one is to ask, observe & respond to. It develops this entrusted knowing of this that you be, to become a willingness to speak into all it is that rises up and is overturned. It feels like you are to start afresh shall we say to offer it as a suggestion to be, to feel willing almost excited to rewrite or cleanse this visionary of old to new. It becomes a divine understanding to express this that you be as excepted and loved. This starts a new discovering of you.

Should I impose any conditions or regulations into this new way to speak?

Why would it feel as to impose upon oneself? Is it not of this agreeance that you are to make to self to be in an honouring state of being to speak? It is the conditions, rules, regulations, and structure that has led you here in this state of disregard and disbelief that you arrived to because of, is it not?

I AM trusting of this new voice?

IN only your desire to do so. In only your confidence and delight to do so. It appears that in this statement to offer that you are still to not trust of this self to speak correct and convincingly of you as. Is this not correct?

You are the stander here in this your NOW.... Take a good long and honest look, of what is it that one is to see?

You are the bystander of all that is to be replicated in this vision of self to have lived, speak, witness, and know.

We speak of a bystander in regard to times of many that you have diligently stood by and allowed another to speak to, over or down upon you. Offering, even shouting dismay and judgment upon all it is that you have felt as you to accept. Being the offeror to this self at times in conversation with this self {being you} that you have taken on as the way it was to describe or condemn yourself.

In human it is we witness many of you acting non-conducively in conversation with each other and self, and this has ruined or deflated your self-esteem to fall into a pitiful state of neglect which overtakes you, dissolving the image of love ever to be seen or held as yours. Registering as inadequate to speak or be ever heard by you or another.

It is in this eliminating of the negating human form and recognising YOU as to be a wonderous contribution in reality to speak of her/ or him as a certainty to know, that the many of you will begin to deafen this irremissible voice that speaks unlovingly, making a space for it to be controlled and encouraged again by this loving voice of reason and right to be never misunderstood as not yours to ever know again.

You speak of By- stander, why is this spoken of as ME?

We suggest here that impression of self is to view of this physical man/ woman as a stander into what they see or think of self to be, does it not?

IN ones willingness to accept, receive and lay upon this form many contributions that are to deflate the energy of love that is yours always in respect of you to be, becomes a deafening way to hear this human as.

In the offering of by-stander we suggest that the many of you upon this earthly planet have stepped outside of the real version of you and have allowed for this walk in to be known as you. It has repressed and depressed the many of you that are or cannot see this self as beautiful and perfectly complete.

These words are hard to accept as mine to speak. WHY?

We catch many of you in a questioning state to rise in regard to words of wonderment to describe this self to be. It is as if to appear a condition upon this planet that you are not equal or never will be to another. It appears that many are in a state of disrepair in regard to the building up or talking up of this self to hear. It appears as a non-allowing or to frown upon when one does, does it not?

Many descriptive words are used to describe of those that do, egotistical, self-boasting, loud mouth, expressor of himself/ herself to be better, out doing, loud, over the top, too much.

Let it be presented here in this topic to cover; that yes it is this that we have spoken of before that in a loud obnoxious way many will attach an ego head to these statements to be heard. Be allowing in ones own truth to speak in love and a proudness attached to the heart that speaks of this self as in a love to grow and encourage, it is a different approach that one must encourage from this human voice to speak of self as entitled and more in a manifestation of self to love and desire to become growth, in comparison to the harsh voice that is to boast outwardly, inconsiderate to all that will listen and assume of self to be above or better than another. In this we wish to describe it is all attached to a lesson of life's self-worth and loved being to be expressed {observe the spoken words and actions of the body to provide clues and acceptances to this observation} and you will witness a reality in all that is a lacking self-worth, self-controlling way, allowing loud, excessive nature to suggest they have, are & do, in a need to prove.

Conditions apply- Do they not?

Ego interaction and enthusiastic involvement?

How does one tell the difference?

Listen to Feel.

Sense difference within one that speaks, feel the contagious energy of love, listen to the way the speaker speaks to portray, rest into one that speaks with passion, quiet to respect, humble to describe in desire and love, eager to hear you, asking, spellbound by simplicity, love spoken.

Being distinguished easily from the one that ego speaks to be heard. Directness, showy, never considering you, one-way conversations, or calling to is an attempt to draw ones observation to the ego psyche that speaks to feel as lacking or not enough; two different statements reveal.

- ❖ I stand in this place, a place of always to dominate, compete and demonstrate my power over you. In all I have, you will hear ME and you will know ME.

❖ The enthusiastic ones speak always in a humble giving way, kindred spirited being, gracious heart to appreciate. Come stand in my light so that WE may shine together.

Mastering the voice, the ego, the self, the human physical state is conducive to LOVE, is it not?

In many we speak these words of love, to be felt as to rise outwardly to be seen, to be felt represented by those that speak of us in this way. Acknowledging the self and others in a way as to approve, not judge and accepting of all that they are to see or be witness to. It eliminates this need to be better than or more of if to word it as so, the loved version of you, the existence that lights you up from within is fluent only in love and compassion.

This is how you will know that you have the ego tamed, be still to speak, accept words offered and allow them to flow, judge not of another in the way that they shall express. All are interpreters of this that they are to know. Seek not to condemn or direct for it is this voice of love that will keep them correct.

Meeting the ego` human.

We feel this statement as an opening from within this human to speak as her own request to ask, it is in a defined being that appears so self-impressed, worthy and in control of all that they be are to challenge thee. YES.... It appears that personalities like this so mentioned are to have it all and feel as to have not one spirited bone within, how can this be.

We speak in a love to be heard that they are not challenged by self-negate, lack to befall them, or to suggest ever that they cannot or will not or wont. It appears to all that witness their unfolding is everything that they desire or dream. To touch turns to gold. It is in this way that one is to step out of the thoughts of as to attach an ego to them to be, for yes they may speak always encouraged by thee, or to support self in every way, see no wrong in all that appears of them to be.

We ask you this; is it ego or not?

Appearance and voice in presentation offers ego to be suggested, but to be a version of human self to be exact in all that they think, say, and do, only encourages more does it not?

These ones appear to be the masters of all that they interpret life as. Attraction to thee. Do they feel no lack of self or appear to not? We question this to regard the reasoning behind how it is they speak, present and disregard.... Delve not to deeply into this as an emotional decision to make for they may simply stir within you an inadequacy to hold deep. Let your observation of them be in only love and acceptance to be, for in all to journey is to meet their own thee. Be told by this that we be, that in all to accept is your learnings to unfold. See never another as this that you are not, for they are all contained descriptively woven into the constraints of this life to be viewed into and of a learning to master the very being of which we describe it to be you.

> You are All this in one unified deciding to become.

Mastering myself seems hard enough, let alone attempting to master another.

One is to never assume the role of master for another, it appears prevalent among your people in this placement of time that you have and will continue to do so, allow, or give credit to those that appear more or higher judged to be spoken of as to master your race/ or this self.

In the deciding to hand to another an opportunity such as this to speak of it distinguishes your powerful resource from within {this be your loved essence to speak as always thy master of self}. It becomes a removal or denoting of this powerful you that you appear to renounce this verified human that you be to think as to be not.

The complications that arise in this scenario to feel controlled or complying to one that rules, suggests a lack of confidence into this that you would suggest as yourself to choose right from wrong and choose inner knowing as your truth, does it not?

It leads to a dictatorship that defines you and all that are caught in this impression of control.

Be spoken of by this self as a loved human in essence to be, to feel empowered by this love that is yours to partake and speak always into, be allowing of all others to express freely without disregard, fear or judgement placed, for this is where contrast and difference is born. Inspiration in self thrives here, bountiful moments of satisfaction to hear truth within oneself. Many are to choose this life to become self-expressed and emotionally attached, to be the variance in this being of life to be produced and played into, leaving oneself sitting to receive many conflicting differences, opinions, and suggestions of this self to assume to be.

We speak this way to portray the variances from external contribution that the many of you are to gain, gather and support this to become an inner knowing of who and what it is that they are to appear to self to be. In many life experiences lived, these opportunities are bestowed upon one to either accept or reject, this leads then into a journey of contribution to self to be felt as to become the recogniser of all that you be and designs the.....

Who or What it is that I AM to be?

Mastering thy self becomes a learning to be known.

> Thy master that lays within ME is mine to cherish, she expresses herself finely and in- tune to ME. I see not to disregard her or argue as to whether she loves me or not. I feel her encrypted in this that I be, this loved being that radiates

outwardly for all that are to see. I know her well and choose this to know, that she will always encourage me to grow, to expand and feel as if to respond to all that I interpret this life to be as mine to know. Be filled from within in this sensing of this uniqueness beloving for ME, I asked to remember this I know and in this remembrance she rose, shining exquisitely divine in this all that I BE. Lessons to interpret and mastery to begin, again in this loved being I shall request all that it is that I am choosing this self to BE, here in this lifetime to receive as a JOYOUS unfolding as mine to know, play and receive into.

Life is a learning, this we guarantee. For it was yours to choose of this to be so.

Belong to you we speak.

In these words, we wish to express that one must become knowing of this self again to be felt as to respond in only an honest contribution to be found as yours to express and to feel again. To know of self is daunting, yes we have heard the many of you that have arrived here to this NOW to speak of self as. Daunted by thoughts of self to be not and to have been not in control of this ones voice and reactions, emotions and thoughts has let you down, has it not?

I ask more on this subject, please.

When one can acknowledge thy self as to be the hearer of all that feels and responds as a right from within, than they begin to cherish this self again, do they not?

It becomes an establishment from within that creates this certainty to know of self well. To feel as to belong to an elite club or group shall we say that allows for this being of love to know that she has, is, and will. In this we wish to expand it becomes a knowing that grows and develops lovingly from within to feel this human that you be speak to self in kind again, as if to have perused all offerings and delving into that has been called forth out of you. In this place of deep respect and forgiveness to this self, the master that lives eternally into and of you is to be never swayed as to respond in an uncaring way but becomes ever to grow into a respectful place to receive, to review and to nurture in all that one feels as to express.

~Revealing the master within~

Revealing your own divine truth.

This divine truth makes its way forward, it lays hesitant it appears in only a thought of yours to be unwilling or scared to hear it spoken outrightly as yours to express. It need never be felt as an unwanted expression for it is yours to know. (In this we offer that many are to recommend this revealing no matter how hard the road feels to travel upon, it is in this that one must do to express truth to be found as yours).

In here you find YOU.

Revealing oneself '*as real*' to yourself let alone another is seen as a task that holds contention and disrupt it appears. It raises many conversations back and forth, and for and against in all that one will feel called to speak. It becomes a determiner from within that feels that it can be honestly heard, not judged, or misguided by the conversationalist that usually holds court within you.

You start to raise your vibration from within, in amongst all this despair and mistrust to be felt as to call out of you this willingness to speak to be heard and to know of who it is that you really are.

Your voice becomes known as this responder into all it is that you are to do, speak and offer. It becomes a place of allowance that you can call as your truthful reality to speak as certain knowing that you respond to as your own guidance.

In kind consideration you become your own 'can do' council within that hears all the for and against but in a deliberate and informed way in which to speak. This is applied to all conversations your own held within and external to enter into. You grow into a place of residency to call self as the master of your thoughts, {this you will} being revealed to this self as the knower of all that you are. In honest conversations and transformed voicing you become the owner of a loved being to stand into to feel as you once again, no longer to be felt as neglected or unheard but to really know in all that you respond into, it is your own.

Master this voice, I will.

Many will feel this statement as an offering of I cannot or will not, why?

In just this way as to respond to self as a MASTER feels as if to be not worthy to call this self the title of master, does it not?

Many of you in human disposition have delved into the realisation of this word to be sensed as greater than, or to be ruler of, or even to attach a religious aspect to the description of MASTER. In this you should, for in this way to express as a word for you to accept it is correct to offer it in all ways as spoken in truth for you to hear.

Let this expert be known by you, as you.

Being reminded in this I am to be, by you.

I AM, mastering this version of me as we speak. It is to be this integration that feels to take place so that I may speak this as ME.

Mastering this version of me enables me to become a voice to hear spoken in love and with love in all versions of this one that I see.

This master that I choose to know as ME is this perfection in right to be.

I enable this voice of mine to speak to me to remind me that I AM a master of self to be.

Honour thy self in this revealing from within that is felt to radiate outwardly in a deliberate deciding to be called your hidden master that lays within.

Honour this master, for he /she is you, in all totality to be called yours.

> You are this honouring are you not?
> Can you feel this to be right within
> you to speak of as your own?

We know the countless numbers of you in human form that have accepted or rejected this opportunity to speak with the divine essence that be encapsulated in you.{ your loving being is the revealed in all that one is to seek}. It is to be an empowerment within this self to feel as to respond to this recognition that reveals this self to you.

> In a choice to be spoken of as yours
> in every right to choose, you will.

Need never be persuaded by another to enter this regal temple of love that houses this very essence of exquisite love to be recollected as yours once more. In all life times it becomes prevalent to this self to fantasise about this exact love, this perfect love, this love that drives one to succeed in self to be, so in this lifetime it is that we admit the many of you will stumble to fall, strive to witness, observe and become, adjust this version of you, transform and encounter many opportunities to train or become, feel awash with emotions, dive deep into this being that you be, reject and complain that you cannot, deliver with purpose all that you are to know, seek out your tribe, enlist the help of strangers to find this that be you, rise above all that you thought self to be, roar, establish this commitment to self to be, react to love, reject love, accept love.

> Know you will grow, expand, and evolve in all these offerings, this you shall.

YOU know this being that is yours to feel from within, let her/ he become the master that you bow to feel, as this love supersedes you in all that you do. It becomes your affirmation, your voice, your trademark, your righted way, your speak, your heart beat to hear, let oneself rejoice in this that you have found.

Mastering Self-love is mine to achieve.

> Claim it as yours accomplished.

This I intend to do. It is in an awareness opening from within that is being revealed to me that I am to be the receiver of this information to believe. Is it not?

In ones allowing of self to believe into all that they are and shall be is a truth that has appeared to have been hidden or neglected even refused by self to come forth. In ones asking of it to be received it shall. Be knowing of this dear ones that you are the mastering that is to become. It has laid dormant or undecided by you as to whether it be yours to speak of self as to hold or own.

A confidence or competence into this being of love that you are to hold internally encrypted and connected to the wholeness that is all to speak of as us. It is in this way that one must be arriving here shall we offer to this place of recognition that it would appear of this self to be satisfied and certain into their path to be revealed over this duration of time to be spoken of as your lifetime.

Time spoken by you is only an understanding for us in this NOW, is it not?

YES, this appears correct to interpret for the many of you have existed into this being of love and light for aeons being called to you to participate into as either physical or not. It has led you here this intuitive being of love and light to be felt expressed by you, for you to comprehend as your soul{ inner voice} to speak.

CHAPTER 14

[I FEEL LIKE] I HAVE ARRIVED

We love this description that follows. To be felt as arrived is an ironic suggestion to speak of this human as. Arrived where we offer to ask?

Being inlaid with this gracious hearted love that you are, to feel like you have arrived is within this self to see & hear the REAL YOU, is it not?

- ❖ To feel this pleasant state of contentment that determines you as no longer needing to seek.
- ❖ Feeling a sense of security and complete within this that you witness self to see.
- ❖ Being felt as to stand into your own power and right to be.
- ❖ Knowing of this one to see worthy and fully satisfied into all she be.
- ❖ Loving yourself grand.

- ❖ Entering into this relationship with spirit, higher self, or god speak to offer as title.
- ❖ Remembering the sovereign being that you are.
- ❖ Experiencing life in this reality and revelling into it.
- ❖ Allowing self to speak her awareness and truth.
- ❖ Revealing to recognise the real ME/ or YOU.
- ❖ Universal recognition and awareness again that you are MORE.
- ❖ Forgiveness to the human/physical, emotional creature that you are.
- ❖ Loving self in ever to express.
- ❖ Attracting well-being, abundance, and joy.
- ❖ Observing all in awash of love.
- ❖ Knowing you are not alone.
- ❖ Growing, expanding, and evolving into all that 'I' shall become.
- ❖ Responding to this heart that speaks.
- ❖ Belief in all this that you BE.
- ❖ Acceptance of ME.
- ❖ Loving myself complete.

`Authors offerings to be felt as her own, to rise on up as a contribution to all that shall ask of them to be their own to speak. Ever expressing these words of love to be felt as hers to receive.

Can you feel to express words or descriptive write to please you?

Be allowing to feel words of love and grace and kind to flow onto these pages as a written script or letter of love for you to receive. It is in this noting of self to ask to receive, be not blinded by the voice of ego or others that are to appear. Permission granted; be yourself, be revealed in an honest acceptance of all that you be. Talk this self-up, envision away and in this you will become the believer into all it is that appears before you to read.

....
....
....
....
....
....
....
....
....
....

Unlimited belief in self

It starts here.... NOW

Why is it that this topic is to scare and send you running for the hills?

To suggest to self to be unlimited or a version of limitless possibilities, becomes a suggestion does it not that feels as if to aggravate or cause concern from within this human to speak such these words of self to be.

Why, we ask? To be heard by you as this to be you must.

I hear you speak as potential to see this I must.

YES, YES ,YES and without a grievance to be felt by you as to how, when or why.

To limit this voice of powerful expression becomes a default that has been allowed to take control and to have been felt as yours to respond into all along, has it not?

It takes courage here we say and of this we know that it is to be portrayed outwardly into a voice that resonates with the sound of gods voice to speak as he does, to feel this infinite wording system that dwells within you known as yours to reconnect back into again.

It is often the eliminator of self to speak that overtakes this spirited version of you that is to only lay in love, only to recognise love for you as you are present in this now to hear. It is the great determiner that you be to live into that you are to feel so unresponsive at times to even hear a voice described in this way as powerful, loving and compassion filled. Feel encouraged here to speak these words of LOVE as they are felt by you to flow.

GIVE IT A TRY

What would it feel like to nurture yourself with a voice that knew no wrong or disbelief?

Can you help determine this for ME?

In ones intuitive self and yes this we agree is shut down in most as in not a need to believe as real or helpful to this that you live.

One must begin to ask this self, has it succeeded you this way as in that you have lived, hidden by voice, or discredited by words spoken or eliminated by this lived in version that is truly not yours to really see. A dishonouring of thy self has been and might still be present and it falls often upon those that are not equipped with this ability to speak of self in this glowing way. For it takes courage we say this it does to hear of ones words to exude love and growth in a way as to feel loved in every way.

Determining this conversation as right or wrong is simply a decision as to of how it shall be done.

In ones choosing to speak or to hear first this voice of LOVE becomes an opening or lit path for you to stand upon. Stand into this self here and now as we speak of what is it that you hear or see?

We ask this of you all often for it is so often a dullened or unheard version to see or hear that we are to feel as the response by you.

Elimination is helpful here to speak of to you.....

To feel this ability within oneself to be not only willing but able to achieve this as a deciding to do one must, it disentangles you from the hidden agendas that have held you so, this powerlessness that has led you, this shallow voice that has held no strength or commitment to you, this vision that has weighed you down as yours to assume, beliefs that are not true in yours to speak of as known as true for you, many we hear their calls of anguish, hurt and heartbroken fears, in this letting go one must for it is often those that hold to tight or are in a place to see no light that we feel as to respond for it is in this way that they are to see of us in the right way. To be not the holders of them to be but to be the offerors to all that ask to receive to know that it is all held within and this they shall receive.

What is it that I must do?

Dear one we get asked this frequently and it is to remind you all that you are this very perfectly placed essence of spirt to be, to be this version of self succeeded in this human to be. You have not failed or been unwilling to see in all reality it was called to you to be this creator of all it was or is that you see. This very version of you that speaks with us now this contribution to humanity to stand in this glorious stance as to speak her truth. Let it be gentle and kind to find these words of love to fill you from inside to feel this intent from self to realise, to remember that you arrived here with this aspect of god shining brightly decidedly so, to be this intricate dust encompassed into all that be, so to feel battered and neglected or judged and unloved is not of what we see.

Speak these words of truth for this they surely are, determine the way that they feel to flow do they hurt and neglect you so? Or do they cradle you and embellish you with love to flourish.

It has been a long-time since I have heard this voice of LOVE.

For many dear one we know of this to be the truth spoken here by you. We ask of you this in who is it that you wish to see? Is it you or another to be?

One must be powerful here in a place as if to resist a limited version of self to see and yes we agree it takes a decided decision to respond to one that has been not loved to be even in a space as if to suggest first to even respond.

Hidden so deeply away forgotten and unheard it feels as if you have had a lot to hide or disagree.

WHY? we ask this of you dear one?

It is in this exact version of you that we see that we are to cherish thee, this response from within that is to speak a truth here and in this now that be you. It takes time this we know but you all arrive in your heavenly truth to speak forth from within to hear as your thy or truth.

Even your why as if to discover that this adventure as you would call life path is revealed to you, to become known by you, to you for you. Let it be this revealing determined from within that feels as if to rob you of your human thoughts as old and unseen for it is this reveal that will rock you so and lead you to feel as though another has taken you over so to speak, this we offer is not so. It is never this to be our intent for in us it is to be spoken of as a respect and love that you are to respond. In this way you will receive all that we be to know that it is you in self to know.

Let us explain more.

Dive deeper here into this that we be, we offer to many that speak of us so, this dilemma that rises out of the human component as to feel as to not know of what or who to call us to be. For it is this you are to receive in your intentions from within to speak to the innerness that be us in you to become as your intuitive voice of love and expansion to belong that your voices are to respond to us in all ways certain and felt by you to name. It is in this defining that we love to participate for we are never hesitant to respond to a name that you so receive to be a calling to us by you to ask. Let this insistent need be way laid as to feel as though you must respond to name or know of us as this direct response as to a human way to lead you down a rabbit warren as if to search and feel your way. This entangles you even more so, for we observe the many of you as you walk with us upon this path of loved light to be yours to speak and the intense response by human mind to catch you up or call you out and lets you feel as if to be deceived by this self to not know of us to speak.

> We are all in every-thing that is
> and not, so to be felt as to need an
> expression of us to speak, let yourself
> connect to your deep loves and let these
> words of reminisce evoke out of you
> this remembering to be yours to receive
> and in this way it is that we will be
> revealed to you to know of us as YOU.

What if 'i' do not hear?

Dear one this we ask you to rephrase,

> I will hear all it is that I require
> to know, for in this voice of response
> to be mine I know I hold the voice of
> love and all that I am within me to
> speak this language of love and light to
> always connect me to this that you be.

Much work feels still needed to be done.

In you dear one this might appear so, but it is in this intention to be felt by you to you that this is not so. You are the surveyors of all it is to see, are you not? This diligence that is yours to aspire to this grand to be is patiently working away under cover it appears for many to realise when and if it is allowed to arise. You are the envisionment that appears from within to speak to know of this human to be so. It is to be told often in true by many and this shall also be you, that you have searched and reached out to all that would listen to this story that you have told as to be so. This we present to you to respond that in this searching and reaching was to have been and it eventually guided you to here, did it not?

Much worry and woe are laid upon this form to speak to this self as to have taken too long and for some it may appear that you are still not there, Where we ask?

CHAPTER 15

ANTICIPATION...

Knowing success.

We offer these words to you to feel as yours to express in this reveal or realisation that starts to unravel from within or (knocks at your door so to speak) it is the excitement that unfolds and grows insistently that becomes of you to start to expect this anticipation.

It is to be felt as a liberation, a revelation, a direct response to be recognising of the inside voice that you have learnt to welcome, asking for it to be felt or heard, to relish in this feeling or emotion if to relate it to the human form to feel. This is your challenging work, your response to self-delving, your shadow work that has unveiled and revealed the real you, the response from you by you to expect only the grand to see this that is you.

How do I know when I am there?

We feel as if to have answered this question repeatedly and received this question often from you travelling upon ones path of discovery or journey, shall we speak; it is in this insistent need to be known by you to this self once more that you will feel this query to rise OFTEN, and in this it will.

Be a considerate responder to this self when one feels this need to ask oneself again,

>AM I THERE YET?
>
>HAVE I SUCCEEDED?
>
>AM I KNOWING?
>
>AM I ME?
>
>WHERE, WHERE, WHERE?

Be a kind and hearted version of this self to speak these words of debate that flow from within the thinker that you are to possess upon this earthly planet to feel as to offer you a thought that just maybe you are not yet.

In ones thinking process and of this we say lays much confusion to the average human to stand into as an observer of all that has and was to have been. It gets confusing in there does it not, we ask? For it is in this way that the many of you are so keen to establish this path of disbelief or I am not yet worthy, I could not be this anticipation in self to receive.

WHY NOT, WE ASK?

```
Of what is it that you have to lose?
```

If one is non-allowing of self to revel in this anticipation and to feel excitement and exuberance at the thought of success to be theirs, then why would it not be as a receiving by you.

We speak often and in many when we offer this to you to receive that one must become the receiver, the joy giver, the ecstatic being of love to crave this version of you. You have done the hard yards it is to say often heard repeated by those of you that are to arrive at this spot.

A decision to see self giddy with glee is an apprehension that many of human embodiment feel as if to face head on and a gritting of teeth are to be bared to all that are to see (this meaning YOU) this wonderment or revealing as it unfolds and is a decision often to be ignored, confronted, and tested (oh boy do you humoids know how to argue with oneself as to the whys and why nots).

Let oneself have the pleasure; just on this one occasion we suggest, to feel this anticipation become yours to steer you into another direction, a direction of forward focus, descriptive interpretation to be read and felt by you once more as the knower of all that you hold into, the magician that you are, the seer of this life as contagious and filled to the brim with a love so bold for you to receive in this establishment of self to be.

You are the knower of this empowerment, are you not?

We often ask this question boldly and matter of factly to the many that stand before us in this place of reasoning to ask.

> YES! is to be the answer that you should offer self to voice, and in this we guarantee that the many of you shall feel a strange pull or sensation from within you to be excited by this response to know it as a truth for you to hear.

Freedom reigns true in your words.

In our words freedom is to always lay, for we do not have resist or disagreeance internally that banishes our thoughts if to be this that you would call our impression to speak. It is in our ever-evolving ability to know of this that we are the success in ALL totality that is that we choose no particular way or description to be held into or onto.

It is in this recognition that we are the receivers, the geniuses of all that IS and is still to be discovered in its knowing that it is already decided as to be.

Simply spoken; we believe.

Welcoming FREEDOM – my new motto.

A GRAND OFFERING TO ONESELF WE CONGRATULATE YOU ON.

It is in this expression, or shall we speak to offer, freedom to speak your truth that will unravel this realisation from within this body of human that you be, that you will find movement, truth, trust, and sureness to succeed.

It is of this that I desire to speak and to experience.

Then you shall.

A common mistake that we are witnessed to, is the observation within this intellect that is yours to delve into, is the inability to receive this easily, this freedom of speech, the receiver of ALL, this REAL YOU.... having been hidden away, ignored, and shunned for way too long has allowed for disbelief to become your first port of call should any- thing wonderful happen or materialise for you.

Why not try it our way for a change, we ask?

In ones endless mad mind battle to be unaccepting of grand, ease and magic to be received as simple as shall we offer - your sun rising in the morning sky....

WHY should it not be!

We ask; Who or What has got in your way?

YOU HAVE!!!!

>>>>> There it is spoken in truth for you to hear as yours, recognise this statement as an acceptance by you to know that it is all in ones thoughts and words delivered inwardly or outwardly that you are to lose this grand vision to see your life as the ultimate attractor.

Believe in you. You carry this magnificent power; for of this it is that you do. You were imprinted with this version of divine attentiveness to thy self, to be a loved being of light that revels in greatness and perfection to be. You are the attractor of ALL that is and in this we wish to speak of as your most achievable desire to be, this that we see as you.

In this becoming it was that you are, to be witness to this interpretation of all that is that you see. Be allowing dear one it is this that we have to speak; you are the asker to receive, to be reminded of this grand being that you are, the acquirer of all that is perceived by you.

Are you following us on this?

Let yourself feel this decidedness to become, be an opening that is to intimidate you at first YES! we speak as a sureness to be felt, for to describe or better still know of this self as an attractor of ALL that it is that one desires is a challenge to believe.

You are this powerful being, you are this inventor, this creator, this realising

into becoming, you are the conductor of
all it is that you desire. Perfectly
in tuned to this limitless energy that
provides, produces, and flows innately into
and of you, so feel as this impression
of YOU begins to change even MORE into a
becoming of an even greater understanding
and belief into a truthful knowing of
WHO & WHAT it is that you really are.

Anticipation is like a drug we offer,
it is an awareness to the human body liken
to no other emotion(addiction), it can
send shockwaves of deliberate fear & angst
as a response to the unknown or unseen or
an intense overwhelming to the thought of
what may be? It becomes an uncertainty
in most does it not to feel this way.

One must become accustomed to this
awareness of anticipation to feel
as it is to fill you with a burning
desire to succeed into all it is that
you are dreaming or desiring of self
to ask, then trustingly receive.

In ones passionate response we say, the
response that entices you, makes you
crave this event, object, or scenario to

reveal, this eagerness that overtakes your every thought, this then becomes a moment of truth for you to feel success and accomplishment into an existence known upon this planet as a 'life well lived' as a 'deserving for you' as a seeing of this envisionment of self to be the entitled version that you asked this self to be.

Are you hooked yet?

It is easy to see why people do become an asker of this state to be known.

If and when one can believe in the magic and potential potency that they possess, they will succeed in any-thing and every-thing that they desire. It becomes ill relevant of size, quantity, or subject to discuss {and of this we have spoken of in and through many that have received this message as this one does} It is a divine placement that guides you, drives you and possesses you at times to feel, for once you stand into this placement of certainty you will know of all this that we speak about.

One must believe in themselves, this is to be felt as the common theme that I am receiving, Is this correct?

YES Dear one, it is always to be recognised in YOU, LOVE and BELIEF into this being of righteousness that you BE, YOU discovered this protentional on a far more deliberate way as to respond into this ALL that you are present into, maybe not upon this earthly knowing as yet, but the aspect of you that is us in all entireties to be you as the all that is.

It is in this unwavering way that one must continue to ask, to be non-faltering in this belief in self to succeed, to gravitate towards always anticipation as to be the receiver of all in all to be.

Be inclined to radiate outwardly a decision to be, to be ever present in this ALL that you are and to observe this self in such a state of AWE and magnificence as to never see no wrong but in only a TRUTHFUL faith and belief into this every-thing for this is YOU dear one, a new perception to view this self as, become acquainted again with this being that IS an entirety to BE ever more always.

I feel as though the old ME has some expanding to do, if she is to carry this newly unearthed power in ME.

Succeed I Will……

Is anticipation an asking or a knowing?

To ask is to receive is it not?

But to know is to be the knower of all that one desires as truth and receivement.

Let this be a gifted understanding into an expression of this self to speak to know of all that one is, is in a certainty to be. So, if one is to be the receiver of this knowledge in this grand way as to be never a contradiction of thought or decision to see this self as the knower of all that one IS; than they shall be always in-tuned to the wisdom of the universe to speak as gods voice to hear.

In an expression of gods voice to speak you are and it is in this way that we desire to describe the inner wisdom that is held deeply within in the many of you that have focused so much energy outwardly searching and striving to convince self and others of another way to succeed as YOU.

STEP 1- It is in the elimination of all outward interactions that one must first instruct this human form to be a believer of and it is in this knowing that one is to become only a listener then to the self that is you.

It is then in,

#STEP 2 - that one must merge into and become an asker to speak, to hear and to navigate this self into and of the ability to see the real you and to feel the truth, trust, and honest reveal of all into this that one is to be to see.

It is a place of unsettlement that can distract even the most resolute at times to feel this disrupt ravage and tear you apart that is to be a place of reckoning to deal with and to call it forth out of you.

But..... in this we offer that is of what one must do, be guided by the intuitive for all reveals are unsettling are they not? For it is in many upon your planet that you are being awakened and reminded of the mistrust that has been imposed upon you as part of this journey to become. It was a solid YES by you in this recognition to be called forth out of you to remember all it is that you are.

Let the fight begin we hear many of you speak.

It is not to be suggested as to be a fight for is this not of what the human that you have been participating into for aeons now? To be the hearer of this real self, the innate chosen gifted being of love that you are. Yes in this we mean she/ he your gifted responder to speak has laid dormant internally thought of as to be but know of this she has been ever present in all interactions known or not. It is simply in this pleasing of self to speak that one will find the response of love as to be the guided intuitive that now speaks for you.

Listen beloved ones we are to offer, for in the ability to listen you will hear this voice so raw and honest to speak as us in you that you will succumb to the motion and energy of this voice to feel a great love, a momentous occasion that causes celebration and rejoice to become apparent in you to witness to see in all that surrounds thee. You are this hearer we now wish to speak to for it is in this listening that one must.

>>>>> We now have your attention

In the ability to surpass all obstacles, and both external and internal commotion and chaos, the countless numbers of you will find this deliberate attempt by others and the minds authority that has held captive you for all of this life so far, will fall away as if to soften and become a dampened state of existence for you to participate into. You will be a willing passenger we offer; to feel the flow of forgivingness and compassion to let you the true seer be the adjuster of all it is that one is to experience.

A new perception will be felt compelled forth out of you as to perceive ones sustainability into as human existence to be.

> You are the receiver, are you not?
>
> You are the asker, are you not?
>
> You are the seer, are you not?

We question you like this as to become a prominent thought or suggestion in and of you to think or ask of self to be.

WHO/ & WHAT is it that I SEE?

If one is to live into a life of excitement, filled with anticipation, expectancy, and joy into what lays ahead to be cherished or received, this in turn becomes a lighted approach to exist into and will fill ones human existence with only freedom and encouragement as to the way life should be.

I feel that you have more to speak on this subject:

Life upon your planet was never meant to be easy it has been offered to us in this way to speak of it as yours to offer.

And in this we are quick to change your point of focus and offer this to suggest.

You are the asker of all to become and eventuate..... YES, YOU!

Let us dispel any thoughts or ideas that you were not the creator of this self to be.

YOU WERE AND YOU ARE.

In this establishment to become you recognised this or these inadequacy's {in this way to offer this word, we do not insinuate failure, lack, or discredit, it is simply to mean growth} within this soul unique to you, and in this doing so you were liberated and loving enough to feel this grand response to befall you to ask to receive all meaningful participations that this one was to require to further this souls expression to develop, to grow, to evolve.

> Look at YOU NOW. Experiencing this realisation that you did, have and are.

In this powerful way you asked, recognised in only love to be felt as you in a totality to be so in this it is that was, is and will be your pathway of discovering this that you are.

Anticipation builds, drags out the suspense, some may even offer it kills.

But be the informant here to express to this self that life is for you, as not only this one individual that you appear to be inhabiting earth as human but in a greater detail to be received as a conscious being of love and light that mingles and interjects with a multitude of many beings just like you. Lit and eternal.

A condensation of all that you are is to be felt as to fit into this human existence of life abound your beautiful planet, is it not?

One must become willing to adjust the human skin shall we say to feel larger than life, grandeur than this human shell and more extravagant than one could ever see this human as.

It is in this way that one must start to speak to self, to expect of this self as the receiver that you are to recognise this gift that you possess.

I really want to ask; HOW do I do this?

By the allowing of this
voice of love to flow.

For it is in this voice of love that
you will hear all that you are.

Your becoming, your reality,
and your totality.

Authentic this voice is when spoken always
in love and hearted speak to feel.

In one and in all, you will find this
script written as encrypted knowledge
of a language that is LOVE.

Cherished by a grander version than
this that one can imagine.

Dear one we offer many attempts are made to interact subtle in most but extravagant in some. It is the timely awareness that you possess in this human that you be to hear this question being asked:

WHO OR WHAT AM I TO BE?

Here we are again back to the original starting point or question it appears.

Lead the way I am to ask of you.

It is not to lead that we must for in many that are recognised in your history recollections or books of knowledge to have been recorded and spoken of this as leaders, or instructors as Kings and Queens of power over the lands and the people and how it was received and executed, has failed you, has it not.

There is no leader nor wiser offering among you or your people that can do this for you, it is a decided implant that has been hidden within you to speak these words of leadership, guidance and reveal only by you as your duty to self to be.

* We speak to many in this way as to be the hearer of this voice in this way as this channel does and it is in her deeper connection to us as us in her that she feels these words as truth to record.

We have spoken in plenty to offer; YOU are the masters of this self, you are the seers of all that you believe, you are the rulers of all that one is to live to realise, you are the wealth that you own. Be of that now. Hear yourself speak this wise wisdom as frank and bold for it is in only you that this leader, and wisdom be known that you all are craving to take control and lead you to freedom....

This wise leader is

BEAUTIFUL YOU.

This one of pure heart,
Thee spirited creature divinely lit within
Feel this response calling
Bellowing and being enticed out of you
Becoming a certainty as yours to speak

Feel recognised here, in this
NOW that you stand

Be the believer in ALL that one sees

Freedom to speak your words of Truth

Know of this as YOU, one must

It is this BELIEF in you where your power
exists to overcome, to accomplish + achieve

You in this earthly suit, deeply
recognised by this love from within is
this sensing of self to succeed, calling
forth to display this YOU as REAL
and LOVED in all that you be.

In this souls presence, this light
of eternal bliss detailed to be

You are this BELIEF

Blessed YOU

~ BELIEVE in YOU~

`We speak always in this as the loving essence of spirited recognition to come forth, to be described as a being of truth and respect of recognition in you as you in all this that we be. It is in this entitled way that we feel our expressing of love flowing freely through this one human in a response to her divine recognition within herself to feel freedom as hers, to speak a truth of just and righteousness to be revealed as us in her words to become a translation into this language of love to be felt by all that are to read her words spoken by us as us to interact as the

ETHERICAL BEINGS
of LOVE & LIGHT

recognised as the `I` in ONE that resides in us ALL.`

I AM AS YOU ARE & IN THIS I TRULY BELIEVE WE WILL FIND LOVE IN EACH OTHER AGAIN.

MORE BOOKS BY AUTHOR TANYA TURTON

Journey Of The Yellow Feather

Beautiful You Within Me

Angels Of Truth We Are

My Heart Speaks

Wanting To Be Me

Honouring Thy Self

Believing in Me

www.ingramcontent.com/pod-product-compliance
Lightning Source LLC
Chambersburg PA
CBHW071955290426
44109CB00018B/2030